W9-ACU-991

THE
SHOSHONE

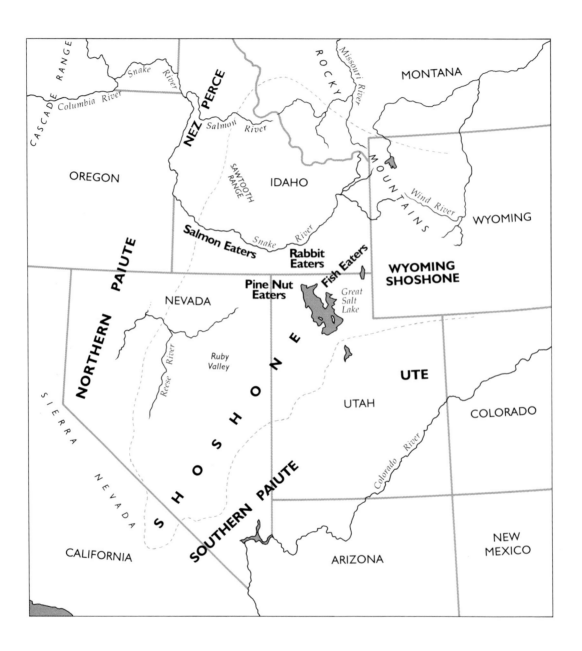

CASCADE RANGE

Snake River

Columbia River

NEZ PERCE

Salmon River

ROCKY

Missouri River

MONTANA

OREGON

SAWTOOTH RANGE

IDAHO

MOUNTAINS

Wind River

WYOMING

Snake River

Salmon Eaters

Rabbit Eaters

Fish Eaters

WYOMING SHOSHONE

Pine Nut Eaters

Great Salt Lake

NORTHERN PAIUTE

NEVADA

Reese River

Ruby Valley

S H O S H O N E

UTE

UTAH

COLORADO

SIERRA

Colorado River

NEVADA

SOUTHERN PAIUTE

CALIFORNIA

ARIZONA

NEW MEXICO

INDIANS OF NORTH AMERICA

THE SHOSHONE

Kim Dramer
New School for Social Research

Frank W. Porter III
General Editor

CHELSEA HOUSE PUBLISHERS
Philadelphia

On the cover   Deer dance headdress of the Idaho Shoshone

Chelsea House Publishers
Editorial Director   Richard Rennert
Picture Editor   Judy Hasday
Art Director   Sara Davis
Production Manager   Pamela Loos

Staff for **THE SHOSHONE**
Senior Editors   Sean Dolan/Jane Shumate
Associate Editor   Therese De Angelis
Editorial Assistant   Kristine Brennan
Senior Designer   Cambraia Magalhaes
Picture Researcher   Patricia Burns

First Printing
1 3 5 7 9 8 6 4 2

Library of congress Cataloging-in-Publication Data
Dramer, Kim.
The Shoshone / Kim Dramer.
    p.   cm.—(Indians of North America)
Includes bibliographical references and index.
Summary: Examines the history, culture, changing fortunes, and current situation of the Shoshone Indians.
    ISBN   0-7910-1687-0 (hc)
              0-7910-4452-1 (pbk)
1. Shoshoni Indians—Juvenile Literature. [1. Shoshoni Indians. 2. Indians of North America—Pacific Basin.] I.Title. II. Series: Indians of North America (Chelsea House Publishers)
E99.S4D73 1996   95-22347
979'.0049745—dc20   CIP
                                                  AC

FRONTISPIECE: *This map shows the distribution of various Shoshone groups across the forbidding Great Basin regions of Utah, Nevada, Idaho, and Wyoming.*

CONTENTS

INDIANS OF NORTH AMERICA

CHELSEA HOUSE PUBLISHERS

INDIANS OF NORTH AMERICA: CONFLICT AND SURVIVAL

Frank W. Porter III

The Indians survived our open intention of wiping them out, and since the tide turned they have even weathered our good intentions toward them, which can be much more deadly.

John Steinbeck
America and Americans

When Europeans first reached the North American continent, they found hundreds of tribes occupying a vast and rich country. The newcomers quickly recognized the wealth of natural resources. They were not, however, so quick or willing to recognize the spiritual, cultural, and intellectual riches of the people they called Indians.

The Indians of North America examines the problems that develop when people with different cultures come together. For American Indians, the consequences of their interaction with non-Indian people have been both productive and tragic. The Europeans believed they had "discovered" a "New World," but their religious bigotry, cultural bias, and materialistic world view kept them from appreciating and understanding the people who lived in it. All too often they attempted to change the way of life of the indigenous people. The Spanish conquistadores wanted the Indians as a source of labor. The Christian missionaries, many of whom were English, viewed them as potential converts. French traders and trappers used the Indians as a means to obtain pelts. As Francis Parkman, the 19th-century historian, stated, "Spanish civilization crushed the Indian; English civilization scorned and neglected him; French civilization embraced and cherished him."

Nearly 500 years later, many people think of American Indians as curious vestiges of a distant past, waging a futile war to survive in a Space Age society. Even today, our understanding of the history and culture of American Indians is too often derived from unsympathetic, culturally biased, and inaccurate reports. The American Indian, described and portrayed in thousands of movies, television programs, books, articles, and government studies, has either been raised to the status of the "noble savage" or disparaged as the "wild Indian" who resisted the westward expansion of the American frontier.

7

Where in this popular view are the real Indians, the human beings and communities whose ancestors can be traced back to ice-age hunters? Where are the creative and indomitable people whose sophisticated technologies used the natural resources to ensure their survival, whose military skill might even have prevented European settlement of North America if not for devastating epidemics and the disruption of the ecology? Where are the men and women who are today diligently struggling to assert their legal rights and express once again the value of their heritage?

The various Indian tribes of North America, like people everywhere, have a history that includes population expansion, adaptation to a range of regional environments, trade across wide networks, internal strife, and warfare. This was the reality. Europeans justified their conquests, however, by creating a mythical image of the New World and its native people. In this myth, the New World was a virgin land, waiting for the Europeans. The arrival of Christopher Columbus ended a timeless primitiveness for the original inhabitants.

Also part of this myth was the debate over the origins of the American Indians. Fantastic and diverse answers were proposed by the early explorers, missionaries, and settlers. Some thought that the Indians were descended from the Ten Lost Tribes of Israel, others that they were descended from inhabitants of the lost continent of Atlantis. One writer suggested that the Indians had reached North America in another Noah's ark.

A later myth, perpetrated by many historians, focused on the relentless persecution during the past five centuries until only a scattering of these "primitive" people remained to be herded onto reservations. This view fails to chronicle the overt and covert ways in which the Indians successfully coped with the intruders.

All of these myths presented one-sided interpretations that ignored the complexity of European and American events and policies. All left serious questions unanswered. What were the origins of the American Indians? Where did they come from? How and when did they get to the New World? What was their life—their culture—really like?

In the late 1800s, anthropologists and archaeologists in the Smithsonian Institution's newly created Bureau of American Ethnology in Washington, D. C., began to study scientifically the history and culture of the Indians of North America. They were motivated by an honest belief that the Indians were on the verge of extinction and that along with them would vanish their languages, religious beliefs, technology, myths, and legends. These men and women went out to visit, study, and record data from as many Indian communities as possible before this information was forever lost.

8

By this time there was a new myth in the national consciousness. American Indians existed as figures in the American past. They had performed a historical mission. They had challenged white settlers who trekked across the continent. Once conquered, however, they were supposed to accept graciously the way of life of their conquerors.

The reality again was different. American Indians resisted both actively and passively. They refused to lose their unique identity, to be assimilated into white society. Many whites viewed the Indians not only as members of a conquered nation but also as "inferior" and "unequal." The rights of the Indians could be expanded, contracted, or modified as the conquerors saw fit. In every generation, white society asked itself what to do with the American Indians. Their answers have resulted in the twists and turns of federal Indian policy.

There were two general approaches. One way was to raise the Indians to a "higher level" by "civilizing" them. Zealous missionaries considered it their Christian duty to elevate the Indian through conversion and scanty education. The other approach was to ignore the Indians until they disappeared under pressure from the ever-expanding white society. The myth of the "vanishing Indian" gave stronger support to the latter option, helping to justify the taking of the Indians' land.

Prior to the end of the 18th century, there was no national policy on Indians simply because the American nation had not yet come into existence. American Indians similarly did not possess a political or social unity with which to confront the various Europeans. They were not homogeneous. Rather, they were loosely formed bands and tribes, speaking nearly 300 languages and thousands of dialects. The collective identity felt by Indians today is a result of their common experiences of defeat and/or mistreatment at the hands of whites.

During the colonial period, the British crown did not have a coordinated policy toward the Indians of North America. Specific tribes (most notably the Iroquois and the Cherokee) became military and political pawns used by both the crown and the individual colonies. The success of the American Revolution brought no immediate change. When the United States acquired new territory from France and Mexico in the early 19th century, the federal government wanted to open this land to settlement by homesteaders. But the Indian tribes that lived on this land had signed treaties with European governments assuring their title to the land. Now the United States assumed legal responsibility for honoring these treaties.

At first, President Thomas Jefferson believed that the Louisiana Purchase contained sufficient land for both the Indians and the white population.

Within a generation, though, it became clear that the Indians would not be allowed to remain. In the 1830s the federal government began to coerce the eastern tribes to sign treaties agreeing to relinquish their ancestral land and move west of the Mississippi River. Whenever these negotiations failed, President Andrew Jackson used the military to remove the Indians. The southeastern tribes, promised food and transportation during their removal to the West, were instead forced to walk the "Trail of Tears." More than 4,000 men, women, and children died during this forced march. The "removal policy" was successful in opening the land to homesteaders, but it created enormous hardships for the Indians.

By 1871 most of the tribes in the United States had signed treaties ceding most or all of their ancestral land in exchange for reservations and welfare. The treaty terms were intended to bind both parties for all time. But in the General Allotment Act of 1887, the federal government changed its policy again. Now the goal was to make tribal members into individual landowners and farmers, encouraging their absorption into white society. This policy was advantageous to whites who were eager to acquire Indian land, but it proved disastrous for the Indians. One hundred thirty-eight million acres of reservation land were subdivided into tracts of 160, 80, or as little as 40 acres, and allotted to tribe members on an individual basis. Land owned in this way was said to have "trust status" and could not be sold. But the surplus land—all Indian land not allotted to individuals— was opened (for sale) to white settlers. Ultimately, more than 90 million acres of land were taken from the Indians by legal and illegal means.

The resulting loss of land was a catastrophe for the Indians. It was necessary to make it illegal for Indians to sell their land to non-Indians. The Indian Reorganization Act of 1934 officially ended the allotment period. Tribes that voted to accept the provisions of this act were reorganized, and an effort was made to purchase land within preexisting reservations to restore an adequate land base.

Ten years later, in 1944, federal Indian policy again shifted. Now the federal government wanted to get out of the "Indian business." In 1953 an act of Congress named specific tribes whose trust status was to be ended "at the earliest possible time." This new law enabled the United States to end unilaterally, whether the Indians wished it or not, the special status that protected the land in Indian tribal reservations. In the 1950s federal Indian policy was to transfer federal responsibility and jurisdiction to state governments, encourage the physical relocation of Indian peoples from reservations to urban areas, and hasten the termination, or extinction, of tribes.

Between 1954 and 1962 Congress passed specific laws authorizing the termination of more than 100 tribal groups. The stated purpose of the termination policy was to ensure the full and complete integration of Indians into American society. However, there is a less benign way to interpret this legislation. Even as termination was being discussed in Congress, 133 separate bills were introduced to permit the transfer of trust land ownership from Indians to non-Indians.

With the Johnson administration in the 1960s the federal government began to reject termination. In the 1970s yet another Indian policy emerged. Known as "self-determination," it favored keeping the protective role of the federal government while increasing tribal participation in, and control of, important areas of local government. In 1983 President Reagan, in a policy statement on Indian affairs, restated the unique "government to government" relationship of the United States with the Indians. However, federal programs since then have moved toward transferring Indian affairs to individual states, which have long desired to gain control of Indian land and resources.

As long as American Indians retain power, land, and resources that are coveted by the states and the federal government, there will continue to be a "clash of cultures," and the issues will be contested in the courts, Congress, the White House, and even in the international human rights community. To give all Americans a greater comprehension of the issues and conflicts involving American Indians today is a major goal of this series. These issues are not easily understood, nor can these conflicts be readily resolved. The study of North American Indian history and culture is a necessary and important step toward that comprehension. All Americans must learn the history of the relations between the Indians and the federal government, recognize the unique legal status of the Indians, and understand the heritage and cultures of the Indians of North America.

A Shoshone Indian village on the south fork of the Little Wind River. This site is now under water as a result of the construction of the Little Wind River.

PEOPLE
OF
THE
GREAT
BASIN

It was Coyote, say the Shoshone, who brought them to the lands of the Great Basin. Coyote was given a basket by two native women, a basket coated with the pitch of pine trees to make it watertight. Coyote was to carry this basket on his journey across the Great Basin—but, the women warned him, he was not to open the lid. Coyote was an inquisitive creature, however, and he could not suppress his curiosity about the contents of the basket. During his journey across the Great Basin, Coyote opened the basket many times to peek inside. And each time he opened the lid, some of the beings inside jumped out. This, say the Shoshone, was how their ancestors came to live in the Great Basin. Ever since Coyote brought them to the land, they have lived in small groups, scattered throughout the basin territory.

Archaeologists believe that about a thousand years ago, a people called the *Numa* came to the lands of the Great Basin from the Southwest. Their migration route can be traced through the presence of their language, Numic, which is a branch of the Uto-Aztecan family of languages. The Great Basin Numa split into three branches—the Northern Paiute, the Southern Paiute, and the Shoshone. Native Shoshone speakers theorize that their name might be derived from *sonippih*, meaning "high growing grass." The name "Shoshone" first appeared in English in the reports of Lewis and Clark as "Sosones or snake Indians." The Shoshone call themselves *niwi*, however, a term also used for "person," with the plural form *niwini* meaning "the people."

The ecology of the Great Basin defined the traditional Shoshone world.

The Great Basin is a vast area between the Sierra Nevada and the Rocky Mountains that makes up almost one-tenth of the land mass of the continental United States. The lands of the Great Basin include all of Utah and Nevada; most of western Colorado; parts of southern Oregon, Idaho, and Wyoming; eastern California; and northern Arizona and New Mexico.

The Great Basin is considered one of the most inhospitable areas of North America. It was formed during the last ice age as glaciers carved beds in the lands of the American West. The beds filled with the cool waters of the melting glaciers and were linked with great rivers teeming with fish. Mammoths and other wild animals grazed the steppes and fertile marshes. Around 10,000 B.C., the climate began to change. As the glaciers retreated north, they took with them their precious store of water. Lakes dried up, streams dwindled, the large animals of the ice age retreated north with the glaciers, and rich woodlands gave way to bristlecone pines and sagebrush. The sun baked the land, shrinking the lakes, which became salt encrusted. What remained was an arid land with strong contrasts between high mountains and intervening valleys running in a north-south direction. The mountains—the Sierra Nevada and Cascade Range—form a rainshadow, blocking the path of rain-bearing clouds that sweep in from the Pacific Ocean. The clouds stack up against the western side of the mountains and release the water they carry there, with few clouds passing the mountain peaks to bring rain to the Great Basin.

Yet this land, largely devoid of fresh water, has supported generations of Shoshone. They call the land *Pia Sokopia*, "Earth Mother," and see themselves in close partnership with it and with the plants and animals with whom they coexist. Their close attachment to the land was described by the historian Hubert Howe Bancroft in 1883: "They are lovers of their country; lovers not of fair hills and fertile valleys, but of inhospitable mountains and barren plains." Their way of life in this seemingly hostile terrain is a masterpiece of adaptation to the environment; according to the noted American anthropologist Robert Murphy, "There are but few known societies in the world that have had to live so close to the margin of survival as the Shoshone." The key to understanding traditional Shoshone culture and its survival strategies is recognizing that spread across the vast and bleak territory are small areas with resource-rich environments—forested mountains, fertile valleys, and stream-fed marshes—around which the Shoshone built their life.

The Shoshone's most important survival skill was their intimate knowledge of the plants and animals found in each of these ecosystems of the Great Basin. They harvested and hunted the seasonal abundance of each microenvironment in turn, plotting their movements according to the availability of each resource, which they used not only for food but also for medicine, tools, and clothing.

The Great Basin landscape of Diamond Valley, Nevada. The Shoshone sustained themselves on this unpromising terrain.

They also learned to adapt physically to the Great Basin's harsh climate, in which the temperature can soar well over 100 degrees Fahrenheit in the summer and fall far below 0 degrees during the winter. To survive this environment, the Shoshone created clothing that ranged from blankets of knotted rabbit fur and special snowshoes in winter to little more than grass aprons and protective pine pitch smeared on their feet in summer.

The Shoshone met their needs for water by making coiled baskets covered with the pitch of pine trees that could store and transport water. This enabled the Shoshone to travel far from water sources to search the land for sustenance. Just like Coyote, the Shoshone crossed the lands of the Great Basin with pitch-covered, water-carrying vessels.

It was precisely the Great Basin's unsuitability for European-style agriculture that kept the Shoshone isolated from outsiders until quite late in American history. Spanish explorers were the first Europeans to see the Great Basin, when, in the late 18th century, they sought routes between Spanish possessions in California and the southern rim of the Great Basin. British and American trappers touched the northern edge of the Great Basin in the early

A Shoshone woman, her shelter, and the landscape seem to blend together as she makes a fire to smoke a hide.

19th century as they sought furbearing animals, but so hostile did they find the region that they scarcely explored it; maps from this period label this area "Mysterious Land" or "Unknown Land." By the middle 19th century the Great Basin was thus the last frontier of the continental United States, and it was so unattractive to American settlers that it was viewed as a place to pass through as quickly as possible on the way to the fertile California coast.

Some explorers, however, entered the Great Basin in search of the legendary Buenaventura River, which was said to originate in the Rocky Mountains, cut through the desert lands of the Great Basin, and empty into San Francisco Bay. Explorers hoped the Buenaventura would afford a quick and easy passage through the hostile lands of the Great Basin.

The explorations of John C. Frémont in 1844 proved that the Buenaventura did not exist: the waterways of the territory did not empty into the ocean. The map from his 1844 expedition notes that the lands between the Wasatch Range and the Sierra Nevada were "surrounded by lofty mountains; contents almost unknown, but believed to be filled with rivers and lakes which have no connection with the sea." Frémont recognized that these lands were a region of internal drainage. The waters flow inward, collecting in depressions like the Great Salt Lake, Pyramid Lake, Humboldt Lake, and Carson Sink. Much of the water passes back into the desert air through evaporation without first being impounded in lakes or marshes. It was Frémont who coined the term "Great Basin" for this immense territory.

In 1858/59, under the auspices of the War Department, J. H. Simpson, a member of the U.S. Army Corps of Engineers, explored and opened a wagon route from the valley of the Great Salt Lake across the Great Basin. Simpson thus shortened the distance between Great Salt Lake and San Francisco by more than 200 miles. In his *History of Explorations*, published in 1869, he described the indigenous peoples of the Great Basin in the most disdainful of terms, as "Indians of an exceedingly low type, who subsist chiefly on roots, grass-seed, rats, lizards, grasshoppers, etc." Other Euro-Americans showed an equally negative attitude toward the Shoshone, whom they called "diggers," a derogatory reference to the Shoshone's practice of digging for edible roots such as camas with simple pointed sticks. Their varied subsistence strategy required them to be ready to move at a moment's notice to a new camp where a food resource was coming into season. For this reason, the Shoshone carried their possessions on their backs and, unlike Euro-Americans, did not alter the landscape with great buildings and permanent dwellings. They left no libraries with hefty tomes to pass on their wisdom and their knowledge. This is why Shoshone culture was often mistakenly described by Euro-Americans as impoverished and primitive.

Today, however, a new sensitivity and concern for the environment has led to a radical reevaluation of the traditional Shoshone way of life. Many scholars have come to the Great Basin to study traditional Shoshone culture, which is now acknowledged as a rational and sophisticated adaptation to one of the most hostile environments in the world. ▲

A Shoshone chief, photographed on the Fort Hall Reservation early in the 20th century. Whites sometimes contemptuously referred to the native peoples of the Great Basin as "diggers" because they foraged for food, but the dignity of this Shoshone belies the disparaging nickname.

MASTERS
OF
SURVIVAL

In order to adapt to any given environment, plants and animals will develop specialized physical features and behavior patterns. For example, in a desert climate, plants such as cacti have adapted by growing broad, leafless stems that use water sparingly because they grow slowly. Animals such as the camel have adapted by conserving water within their bodies and developing feet with broad, thick, calloused soles suitable for desert travel. Human beings, on the other hand, survive principally by adapting their behavior and by manipulating the physical landscape. The Shoshone used many strategies to ensure survival in the harsh environment of the Great Basin.

Water was the most important resource the Shoshone had to manage, for without it, a person cannot survive for even a week. To allow them to store and transport water on their frequent journeys, Shoshone women—who were skillful basket makers and developed a variety of specialized vessels for winnowing, gathering, and storing foods—wove coiled baskets. They then collected the resin of the piñon pine tree, heated it until it liquified, poured this liquid pine pitch into the tightly woven baskets, and swirled it until it completely coated the inside. The result was a light, waterproof vessel that allowed the Shoshone to travel great distances throughout the Great Basin without fear of thirst, in a sense mirroring Coyote's original journey.

With their water supply secure, the hunter-gatherer Shoshone developed a way of life in which they traveled throughout the Great Basin to each scattered ecological niche in turn, relying upon their intimate knowledge to gather the distinct resources each offered according to the season. Such microenvironments could only sustain a small number of inhabitants, however, so the Shoshone traveled in groups usually no larger than an extended family. The Shoshone in fact referred to specific groups according to each one's principal land or diet. Grouse Creek Shoshone were called *tipatikka*, "eaters of pine nuts"; the Lemhi Shoshone, living in the Lemhi River valley and along the Upper Salmon River, were called *akaitikka*, "eaters of salmon"; the Reese River band were called *mahaguadüika*, "eaters of Mentzela seeds"; Shoshone of the Ruby Valley were known as *watatikka*, "eaters of ryegrass seed"; and those of the Smith Creek valley were *kuyatikka*, "eaters of bitterroot."

The Shoshone visited dozens of small sites during their yearly rounds, occupying them only briefly because their limited resources could not support large populations for long. These were areas where animals such as antelope and jackrabbit might be hunted, where salmon might be fished during their migration to the sea, or where ripened seeds and roots might be collected. In the late fall, however, many Shoshone groups traveled to villages in the mountains for an extended stay to harvest the ripened seeds of the piñon trees—for these seeds, pine nuts, were by far the Shoshone's most important plant resource. Highly nutritious and abundant, the nuts are 54 percent carbohydrate, 23 percent fat, and 10 percent protein. It has been estimated that a Shoshone family of four could gather 1,200 pounds of pine nuts during the fall nutting season, and this supply would provide food for four months.

Modern botanists have proven that the pine, like the first humans in North America, reached this continent from Asia; it then spread as far south as Mexico. Then, 60 million years ago, during the Paleocene epoch, North America was the scene of a great drought, in which only hardy, drought-resistant plants could survive. The arid landscape led to new forms of plant life, and the piñon pine was born—a short-trunked tree that uses water sparingly, takes 75 years to mature, and produces nuts for up to 400 years.

The Shoshone had their own story about the origin of the piñon trees in the Great Basin. The nuts are said to have come from a northern location during the autumn, when the north wind was blowing. It was then that Crow, with his keen sense of smell, detected the scent of roasting pine nuts on the north wind, and he began to choke and vomit blood. The shaman could not help his mysterious ailment, but Coyote solved the mystery of Crow's illness: he told the Shoshone of the piñon trees and their harvest of rich pine nuts to the north.

The Shoshone decided to get the Main Seed of the piñon. They traveled north, where the Pine Nut Eaters welcomed them to join in their dancing and games during the piñon harvest. Field Mouse succeeded in stealing the Main Seed hidden in the highest tree. Then the Shoshone fled south with the Main Seed, and the Pine Nut Eaters ran after them.

Crow hid the Main Seed in his

thigh, wished his leg to become infected, and wished that Crane would kick it and then temporarily lose his mind. Then Crow died. Crane came to Crow's body and kicked his infected thigh, which, with its hidden Main Seed, flew off into the mountains. Crane was confused and dizzy, so he sat down facing north. When Crane's mind cleared, he looked for Crow's thigh but could not find it. Crane and his friends then looked to the south. They saw piñon trees growing on the mountains; they smelled the roasting pine cones. For this reason, the Shoshone say, the red coloring in the mountains to the south looks like blood, for it was here that Crow choked and vomited blood. To this day, the Shoshone say, they are warned by their elders to sit quietly when they eat pine nuts so they will not choke.

Each fall, the Shoshone continued to travel to the mountains, where they established piñon villages to harvest the pine nuts. Shoshone settlement patterns as well as religious and social life were influenced by the importance of the pine nut, for the fall gathering was not only a time of harvest, but also a time of celebrations and circle dances. Because the piñon trees were thought to have spirits residing within them, many special religious rituals were observed to show respect to the spirits of the trees and ensure continued bountiful harvests.

The piñon villages were located in the ecotone—a transitional ecological zone—between the sagebrush flats and the piñon-juniper belt. The villages

Plant fibers were used by the Shoshone to make vessels for holding water and other liquids, such as this twill-twined water bottle. Piñon resin was used to seal such vessels and make them watertight.

were not situated near streams, since the Shoshone did not wish to scare away game animals that would come to drink at the streams and would then be hunted to supplement the Indians' diet. Water was instead supplied by snow on the ground. The Shoshone were well aware of competition for the piñon nuts from piñon jays, chipmunks, wood rats, and piñon mice, so they timed their visits to the trees to arrive ahead of these animals and harvested the cones before they opened and exposed their seeds. To

The single-leaf piñon, Pinus monophylla, *is virtually ubiquitous in the Great Basin region. The name* piñon *is Spanish and refers to the large, edible seeds of certain pine species. These seeds were a staple of the Shoshone's diet for thousands of years.*

do this, the Shoshones developed special implements and systems.

The green cones of the piñon tree were gathered with long, hooked harvesting poles, placed in conical baskets, and transported to a site where large pits had been dug and filled with burning charcoal embers. The green cones were roasted in the pits, causing them to open and expose the piñon nuts. Next, Shoshone women beat the cones with sticks to release the seeds, which were collected in fan-shaped trays and parched in a fire to make the seed coats brittle. The shelling of the piñon nuts

was also the work of women, using a flat stone slab called a *metate* and many special types of hullers. The nuts were parched over the fire a final time in circular trays.

The seeds were now ready for grinding to make mush or gruel, a favorite dish of the Shoshone. The women ground the nuts on a metate with a loaf-shaped stone called a *mano* to produce meal. The meal was mixed with cold water in a special basket called a mush basket. The women used a looped stick to stir the mixture. Some Shoshone ate the mush cold, while other groups cooked the mush by stone-boiling: adding heated rocks to the mixture in the mush baskets in order to cook it. In areas where cold temperatures made freezing possible, mush baskets were set outside to make a sort of piñon ice cream—a favorite of Shoshone children.

The Shoshone, always mindful of the unpredictability of the weather and the availability of resources in the Great Basin, used this time of plenty to store food for the hard times they knew would come. They stored seeds that had been partially processed in skin bags or pits lined with grass or bark, and they buried some piñon cones in large pits with a covering of rocks, tree limbs, and pine needles; seeds stored in cone caches could keep for four to five years.

Each autumn, after the Shoshone had assembled in their piñon villages, they organized communal rabbit hunts. The Shoshone depended heavily upon rabbits for meat to supplement their winter supply of pine nuts and to provide furs for warm winter blankets. Both jackrabbits and cottontails were taken in communal drives that employed large numbers of people from many bands and that were led by hunting specialists called "rabbit bosses."

Nets were set in semicircular or V-shaped formations. Men, women, and children worked their way through the brush of the valley bottoms, driving the rabbits before them. The object was not to snare the rabbits in the nets, but to prevent their escape so the Shoshone men could club them to death or shoot them with bows and arrows. The nets were heirlooms, passed down from generation to generation. If a rabbit became entangled, it would damage a net, which would take a long time to repair.

The rabbits were then skinned, split, and dried for winter storage. Some were pit-roasted whole or cleaned and stuffed with wild onions before cooking. The animals' fur was cut into thin strips that were dried and curled under in the hot sun. The result was a sort of fur rope, many of which were then knotted together to make winter blankets; it took about 100 rabbit skins to make a fur robe for a Shoshone adult. Wrapped in their rabbit robes, with their water supplied by snow and their food resources of rabbit meat and pine nuts secure, the Shoshone passed the harsh Great Basin winters.

In the spring and summer, the Shoshone harvested roots, seeds, berries, and leaves. Shoshone women were expert at identifying hundreds of

The Shoshone made dishes and trays from fibers, rather than from clay or fired materials, as was done, for example, by the native peoples of the Southwest. This particular tray was used for winnowing and drying foodstuffs.

plants, some growing in the foothills, some in the marshes, and others at higher elevations. Roots, ferns, fruit, seeds, berries, and nuts were harvested for food; seeds from wild grasses such as rice grass and ryegrass were used as grain; and several sagebrush species provided fiber for baskets.

Curved digging sticks of hardwood were used to gather camas, swamp onion, and edible valerian, which could be eaten raw or cooked. Root harvesting was especially important in the northern areas of the Great Basin, as this area

Conical and triangular forms were characteristic of Shoshone vessels, such as this carrying basket, which was probably used for piñon nuts.

is on the fringe of the Columbia Plateau and is well supplied with biscuit roots, tampa, bitterroot, and camas.

Berries and other fruits were harvested throughout the Great Basin area by Shoshone women and children who worked efficiently by using specialized baskets. Each harvester wore a small twined basket that hung around her neck and lay across her chest. She used both hands to quickly fill the basket, and when it was full, she emptied it into a larger basket that was on her back, suspended from her shoulders. Berries were eaten fresh or sun-dried whole and stored in pits and bags for future use.

Fresh leaves were also harvested and eaten raw, boiled, or stored for use in medicinal teas. The stalks of cattails and thistles were peeled and their inner pith eaten. The Shoshone also ate desert plants such as mesquite and screwbean. In the spring, the pods of mesquite were eaten raw as snacks. In the late summer, after the pods had dried, the Shoshone women harvested them, placed them in large mortars made of the stumps of cottonwood trees or carved directly in the bedrock, and, with large cylindrical pestles, pounded the pods into a fine powdery meal. The meal was packed tightly in cone-shaped baskets and left to dry. The baskets were stored in pits lined with grass or bark or in cool rock shelters and caves. The Shoshone kept a cone of the meal at hand to eat alone or to use as a flour for sweet cakes made from cooked agave.

Agave was found in the southern deserts of the Great Basin. In the spring, the Shoshone gathered the plants by using a special knife or chisel-shaped wedge made of wood to cut the leaves from their roots. The leaves were then trimmed and pit-roasted for 24 hours, after which the agave was a sweet, dark mass. Each family cooled and pounded the agave to form large, flat cakes. The agave could be mixed with other types of meal or with game to make a stew.

Indian rice grass and other seed-head crops were harvested with sticks of hardwood and collected in baskets. The seeds were parched using heated stones on woven trays. The heat caused the husks to open and release the edible kernel. Tossing the seeds lightly separated the edible seed from the husks.

In addition to gathering plants for food, the Shoshone also used many species—more than 300—medicinally. Shoshone women were particularly renowned as herbalists, and their intimate knowledge of Great Basin plants accorded them equal status with men. They knew, for example, that cuts and wounds would respond to a mash made of cedar pitch; that Oregon grape was good for eye ailments; and that snakeweed helped treat intestinal ills.

Despite their vast knowledge of Great Basin plant life, the Shoshone did not practice true agriculture. They did, however, develop various techniques to encourage the growth of favored plants. They burned patches of growth to increase tobacco and wild seed harvests as well as to provide fodder for game such as deer and antelope. The Shoshone also scattered seeds of lamb's quarter, stick leaf, and Indian rice grass on these burned patches of grasslands, though "managing" wild plants in this way is not true agriculture. Recognizing the advantages of pruning plants to achieve a greater yield, the Shoshone broke the tips of piñon branches so they would produce more cones in subsequent years.

Whereas women possessed knowledge about plant resources, men possessed special knowledge about ani-

mals, which were likewise crucial to Shoshone survival. Bighorn sheep ranged the Great Basin from the valley floor to the canyons and mountain peaks, and the Shoshone developed a variety of methods for hunting them. An individual sheep might be stalked by a lone hunter, or groups of sheep were ambushed along favorite trails, with dogs driving them toward waiting hunters. Nooses and net snares were also used. Sometimes, Shoshone hunters would disguise themselves in the skins and horns of young male animals to gain an advantage. Hunters would beat logs to imitate the sound of rutting battles—fights between males for females during the mating season—to attract sheep toward their arrows.

The meat of the sheep was prepared by the women, who might barbecue it on long sticks, cook it in rock-lined pits, or fill the body cavity of the sheep with water and add hot stones to cook it from within. Some meat was cut into thin strips for drying, then pounded and mixed with berries and fat to make pemmican.

Deer and pronghorn were also hunted by a variety of methods. The animals were stalked and killed by Shoshone hunters using arrows. To ensure a kill, the hunters dipped the arrows in poisons such as rattlesnake venom, rotted entrails or blood, or the juice of poisonous plants. An animal wounded with a poisoned arrow was tracked until it died or until the hunter could deliver a fatal shot. As with hunting sheep, sometimes a hunter would

Shoshone dwellings were quite similar to those devised by the Plains Indians.

don a deer skin and horns and move carefully to within shooting distance or strike deer antlers together to attract other animals.

In suitable areas, the Shoshone also employed group hunting strategies. The animals would be corralled in narrow canyons or at certain places along migratory trails the Shoshone knew well. Corrals were constructed of the materials at hand, usually brush and rock. Some hunters would drive the animals into the corral with shouts and gestures while other hunters acted as bowmen and shot the entrapped animals.

Another group strategy was to drive the animals along a trail across which the Shoshone hunters had built a low brush fence. As the animals jumped the fence, hunters hiding in a pit behind the brush shot them. Sometimes the brush was set on fire to drive the animals. The burning of brush had another advantage for the Shoshone: it improved the forage for game during the next season by increasing the number of certain favored plants.

The Shoshone also captured birds. They used nets, sometimes first disguising themselves in antelope skin and horns so as not to alarm the birds, then flushing them into the nets. Communal drives of waterfowl depended upon the use of decoys constructed of twined tules (bulrushes) to give them buoyancy. The tule frame was covered with the skin and head of a bird, which was attached to the frame with wooden pegs. Hidden by the decoys, the hunters then drew close to the waterfowl and drove them into nets or shot them with arrows. Another strategy was to place a mound of tules resembling a beaver's lodge over the head of a hunter, who then swam through the water and pulled the ducks under by their legs. The hunter might also wear a duck-skin helmet, swim under the surface using a tube of cane as a breathing apparatus, sneak up on the birds, and pull them under. The Shoshone ate the birds fresh and collected their eggs, which they added to stews and mushes or basket-boiled with hot stones. Eggs could be preserved by being buried in cold sand.

In addition to hunting game and fowl, the Shoshone fished the streams and lakes of the Great Basin using many different techniques. Runs of oceangoing salmon in the Snake River and its tributaries were an important source of food for the Shoshone, who constructed weirs (enclosures) to channel the fish toward waiting harpooners. The harpooners tried to spear mainly the male fish to assure regeneration in the spawning beds. Women also used the flat, open parching trays from the piñon-nut harvest to scoop tiny fish from the water. These were dried in the sun and pulverized to be added to soups and stews.

In the southernmost areas of the Great Basin, the Shoshone captured reptiles and insects for food. They hunted large lizards such as chuckwallas in the crevices of rocks, using pointed bones attached with pitch to long wooden poles. When the Shoshone hunter spied the lizard, he inserted the stick into the rock crevice and twisted it to secure the animal. They also sought desert tortoises, which were roasted in the fire and eaten. To catch grasshoppers, the Shoshone built trenches into which the insects were driven by fire or by a group of beaters. The grasshoppers were parched in woven basket trays and then ground into meal to be added to soups and stews.

The Shoshone way of life could work only for those who had an intimate knowledge of the environment and the animals and plants within it. But the fact that any given resource might not appear in abundance during a particular season was a constant threat to survival. Because the Shoshone believed, however, that the spirits who inhabit the earth and sky would provide for them if proper respect and thanks were shown, they developed a rich and complex spiritual life to help ensure their survival. ▲

Clay figurines of the peoples of the Fremont culture, ancient Great Basin ancestors of the Shoshone. The Shoshone regarded such figurines and the cave drawings made by the Fremont people as the handiwork of the spirits.

SPIRITUAL
LIFE

The natural world of the Great Basin provided the Shoshone with both their means of survival and the basis of their spiritual life. Piñon trees and sagebrush, coyotes and wolves, rivers, rocks, mountains, and even the stars played a role in the religion of the Shoshone. They believed that they were in constant contact with the spirits inhabiting the Great Basin and that these spirits, together with all the elements of the natural world, cooperated to create a harmonious universe. The Shoshone sought the help of the spirits in obtaining game, ensuring the seasonal growth of Great Basin plant resources, defeating enemies, and curing ailments. In return, the Shoshone observed rituals and taboos to show respect and gratitude to the spirits for their help. Thus the underlying philosophy of the Shoshone religion was that respect for the spirit world was rewarded with good fortune.

Each Shoshone hunter, for example, developed a personal relationship with the spirit world and had rituals and strategies to appeal to the spirits and ensure his hunting success. There were magic practices that would help bring game to a Shoshone hunter's hand: for instance, when he found deer tracks, he placed blood in them, which he believed would help tire the animal so it could be stalked more effectively. While individual hunters developed their own rituals, certain Shoshone were believed to have special bonds with particular animals; highly valued by the community, these men were called hunting specialists, and they led communal hunts for antelope, bighorn sheep, and rabbit.

The idea of the special bond these men held came from the belief that humans and animals had been linked ever since the world was created—a time when animals spoke a human tongue and thought human thoughts. The Shoshone believed that Wolf had created humans and that Wolf's younger brother, Coyote, had brought them to the Great Basin. In many Numic-speaking groups, Coyote is still called "our father's brother"; Bear is called "our father's sister"; and Rattlesnake is called "our father's father."

Those Shoshone who were believed to have special bonds with particular animals received their powers from the spirits during a vision quest. During such a quest, a single Shoshone male rode out to the foothills of the Great Basin to seek contact with the spirits. The foothills are the site of petroglyphs, or rock drawings, that archaeologists have attributed to members of the Fremont culture, a group that reached the Great Basin about A.D. 400, grew crops, and built small villages. About a thousand years ago, their culture disappeared from the Great Basin and was replaced by the ancestors of the Shoshone. For the Shoshone, however, the drawings were made by the spirits of the Great Basin themselves and are pictures of the supernatural world. The drawings emitted powerful forces that the vision seeker could feel.

Before setting out on his vision quest, a Shoshone purified himself by bathing in a creek or lake. As a sign of respect, he approached the foothills barefoot, wearing nothing but a blanket, and carrying no weapons, food, or water. Under the open sky of the Great Basin, he lay on the ground without eating or sleeping and waited for signs of favor from atmospheric powers such as lightning and winds or from nature spirits associated with plants, animals, mountains, and lakes.

First, the spirits sent trials of danger for the seeker to overcome. An animal might approach the lone, unarmed Shoshone: a coyote might try to bite him or a rattlesnake might coil up near his body. If the vision seeker showed that he was unafraid and spiritually strong, the spirit would then make a mysterious appearance before him in the form of an animal. During this visit, the vision seeker and the spirit entered into a partnership, in which the spirit would transfer special power to the man: a beaver spirit might transfer strong swimming ability to his Shoshone brother; a magpie might endow the seeker with the talents of a good scout; an antelope might give the power of swift running.

The seeker would be instructed by the spirit on his obligations in the partnership, which might include rules of dress, such as the wearing of feathers, a deer tail, or an antelope hoof. The spirit might teach him a sacred song or set down rules for things the seeker must now avoid as taboo. And the vision seeker had to listen attentively, as careless use of his new powers meant that he had no respect for his spirit. A viola-

Fremont-like figures drawn on the wall of Horseshoe Canyon.

tion of any of these rules or a neglect of a ritual could result in the loss of his power and punishment for his transgressions: he might have bad luck, an accident, or fall ill as a result of his lack of respect. Attentiveness, however, might attune the seeker to the ways of animals and make him a hunting specialist, enabling him to lead the communal hunts and play a crucial role in the well-being of his people.

During communal hunts of rabbit or pronghorn, hunting specialists, with their special powers, were called upon for their skills. Such men enjoyed great status; pronghorn specialists were believed able to call the pronghorn to the hunters and keep them spiritually captive until they could be killed. These hunting specialists slept among the herd for several nights, singing to the animals to strengthen their powers.

The pronghorn specialist carried a gourd decorated with antelope hooves, which he shook near the pronghorn. He sang a song that ended in the imitation of antelope sounds and was believed to attract the animals. While the specialist worked his powers among the pronghorn, other Shoshone hunters carried

These Great Basin petroglyphs were drawn on rocks near the Carson River in Nevada thousands of years ago. The Shoshone regarded figures such as these as evidence of the truth of their religious beliefs.

out practical steps for the hunt. They constructed a corral made of brush or held a heavy sagebrush rope in a large circle. Once the specialist had done his work, the animals were herded into the enclosure and were run until they tired. Then Shoshone hunters entered the enclosure and shot them with arrows or clubbed them to death.

Because the partnership of the Shoshone with the animals involved a set of obligations and rights, rituals were performed after the hunt. Once a large bighorn sheep or antelope was killed, the animal was placed with its head to the east and addressed with great respect by the hunters. Shoshone hunters would offer the eyes and skulls to the spirits by setting them out in the brush, burying them, or suspending them from trees. Because the Shoshone were well aware that many resources in the Great Basin were cyclical and that the pronghorn population needed time to repopulate, these pronghorn hunts took place only every 5 to 10 years.

Just as the spirits of animals helped ensure the spiritual and physical well-being of the Shoshone, so too did the spirits of plants. Many plants played major roles in Shoshone religion. Rabbitbrush, for example, was burned for purification, and big sagebrush was crushed in efforts to contact the spirit world: its pungent odor was believed to carry messages to the spirits asking for their help in ripening pine nuts or curing illnesses.

Like hunting, the taking of plants was accompanied by taboos and rituals, and certain women—such as those who oversaw the roasting of agave and the harvesting of pine nuts—were believed to have special bonds with the plant world and so were entrusted to perform these ceremonies. Offerings to plant spirits were made, and singing and dancing took place to celebrate, give thanks for, and ensure success in obtaining plant food.

Some Shoshone vision seekers received special powers from the spirits that allowed them to cure illness. Euro-Americans have labeled such Shoshone "medicine men," but this concept was foreign to the Shoshone, who instead called such men *puhagan*, meaning possessors of power. These men were called in to treat a patient after well-known plant remedies did not work. Some puhagan specialized in particular maladies such as rattlesnake bites or pneumonia.

The Shoshone believed that some ailments—including infections, aches, and internal diseases—were caused by sorcery, the breaking of taboos, or the anger of the spirits. When this was the case, the specialist sought to remove the dangerous spirit or object that had entered the patient by sucking it out or by brushing or blowing it away with feathers.

In more serious cases, the cause of illness was believed to be the departure of the patient's soul. The Shoshone believed that the soul could leave the body by passing through a hole in the crown of the head, which caused high

Northern Shoshone pose with a type of drum used for the Grass Dance and other religious ceremonies. During the actual ceremony, this drum would likely have been suspended above the ground by four support stakes holding the instrument's rawhide handles. This was done to give the sound of the drum greater resonance.

fever or coma. In these cases, the curer had to travel to the land of the dead and retrieve the patient's soul. This was a difficult and dangerous journey, which the puhagan could make by going into a trance. Then he sent his own soul to locate and bring back the soul of the patient.

To perform his cures, the puhagan was assisted by an interpreter and used incantations and songs, learned at a secret place when the puhagan first obtained his spirit powers. The puhagan forgot the songs until they were needed at each ritual, however, and the interpreter's job was to translate and comment upon the curer's songs. Then the audience understood the songs and participated in the singing and cure.

Thus the Shoshone had a rich set of beliefs about the spirit world, the natural world, themselves, and how all the elements fit together to form a harmo-

nious universe. They believed both good and bad luck resulted from a person's ability to uphold his or her obligations in maintaining this harmony. In return for respect, the spirits sent each resource to the Great Basin in season, and this bounty gave form to the Shoshone year. Generation after generation, the Shoshone roamed the Great Basin following the cycle of food resources upon which their survival depended.

Although the Shoshone had this rich culture, they lacked a written language. Thus they passed their knowledge of the spirit and natural world from generation to generation by means of stories. Around the smoking fires of the piñon villages each year, the elders told stories that shaped the traditional world of the Shoshone, in which spirits and people walked side by side. ▲

A Shoshone woman with her child in a baby carrier.

THE
SHOSHONE
CIRCLE
OF
LIFE

The annual piñon harvest gave focus to the traditional Shoshone year. At the previous fall's piñon festival, the Shoshone would have made arrangements for the following year's piñon village. It takes three growing seasons to produce pine nuts ready to be harvested, and the green pinecones are visible for about 15 months before maturity. The Shoshone noted which piñon groves had the most green cones and so knew at least a year in advance which piñon trees would offer a plentiful supply of nuts. Each family offered information on a good location, and the group then decided upon the area they thought would be the most fruitful.

When the Shoshone families gathered at their new piñon village, they constructed huts to pass the winter. A typical Shoshone winter hut was built by forming a ring of stones to support walls made of poles. These poles were woven together with reeds or bark twine and covered with earth, grass, bark, and brush. The completed structure resembled a cone without a tip. In the center of the hut burned a brush fire, whose smoke escaped through a hole in the roof. A windbreak of brush was constructed to shelter the huts from the fierce winter winds.

From 2 to 10 families passed the winter together in each piñon village. A Shoshone family of about six or seven people—two children, their parents, a grandparent, and perhaps an unmarried aunt or uncle—would spend the winter in one hut.

During the day, the Shoshone men prepared hunting equipment. Many hands were needed for this work, and children helped with the tasks. Shoshone men would manufacture knife blades and arrowheads using a method called flint knapping—striking smaller stones with a large hammer stone to produce fractures with sharp edges. By skillfully aiming the blows of the hammer stone, the hunter could produce an arrow in about 20 minutes. Dull knives could be sharpened by running a piece of horn or antler across the edge of the blade to produce a fresh, smooth cutting edge. Shoshone men also repaired rabbit and fish nets used in communal hunts, and they made bows and notched and feathered arrows.

While men prepared for the hunt, Shoshone women made food, clothing, and baskets. They hulled and roasted pine nuts—a long process in which young girls lent a hand; they made pine-nut mush; and they cooked nourishing stews of pine nuts and game, adding dried fruits from the summer's harvest for flavor. The women knotted rabbit-skin robes to keep their families warm during the winter; and they wove baskets. Under their skilled hands, bowls, cups, ladles, and trays were quickly constructed. Baskets for gathering and transporting food were made in specialized shapes such as the gathering basket, the burden basket, and the berry basket. Water-carrying baskets and canteens were made and waterproofed with pitch. Shoshone women knew how to make pots from clay, but they preferred the light, unbreakable baskets that were perfect for their wandering way of life.

Shoshone women decorated many of these objects with geometric designs, paying particular attention to treasure baskets and cradles. The women applied decoration using plant fibers or overpainting with mineral pigments. Shoshone baskets were prized by other native peoples and traded in a network that crossed the Rocky Mountains all the way to the Pacific Ocean. The beautiful Shoshone baskets were traded for obsidian (a black volcanic glass) to make arrowheads and knife blades, for buffalo skins, and for shells from the California coast. The Shoshone were happy to obtain beautiful shells for earrings and necklaces in exchange for their baskets.

At night, after the piñon harvest, entire families gathered around fires for storytelling. The Shoshone term *natik-winappi* literally means "telling each other stories," which refers to the participation of the audience in Shoshone storytelling. As the elders recited each tale, family members provided responses or questions during set pauses in the story. The elders told tales of creation, morality, magic, and courage. These stories, passed from generation to generation, both educated and entertained; the themes were both spiritual and worldly.

There were tales of an underground world populated with people and animals. When it was day on earth, it was night underground, and vice versa; the entrance to this world was through the caves found throughout the Great Basin. There were cautionary tales about women and children abducted by the hostile groups surrounding the Shoshone in the Great Basin. These tales warned Shoshone of the danger of being kidnapped, inspiring them with the courage of the victims and enter-

Canvas tipis such as these were common Shoshone winter dwellings. The sagebrush gathered and piled behind and around the tipis was intended to serve as a windbreak. The high-wheeled wagon (right foreground) was a common means of transportation for the Shoshone from the 1880s until the 1940s.

taining them with the inventive ways the captives escaped and found food and water on their homeward journeys.

Other stories, telling of a landscape populated by supernatural beings, explained accidents or illnesses. *Paohmaa*, or Water Baby, was an evil spirit who lived in springs or lakes and stole babies or pulled people into the water. *Minimpi*, the dwarf mountain man, roamed the Great Basin armed with a bow and invisible arrows that could cause sickness in animals and people; the Shoshone explained tuberculosis as the result of being shot by one of Minimpi's arrows. And a giant ogre called *Tsoavits* lived in the Sawtooth Mountains in south-central Idaho, which the Shoshone called *coapiccan kahni*, or "the giant's house." He wandered alone across the Great Basin, and when he came upon a human, he paralyzed him with his terrible glance, caught him with a hook like those used by Shoshone hunters to capture chuckwallas, and carried him off in a gathering basket such as Shoshone women used to harvest berries. Many Shoshone thought the basket was lined with thorns. The unhappy victim was taken back to the giant's house to be eaten. Fire, the Shoshone thought, was the

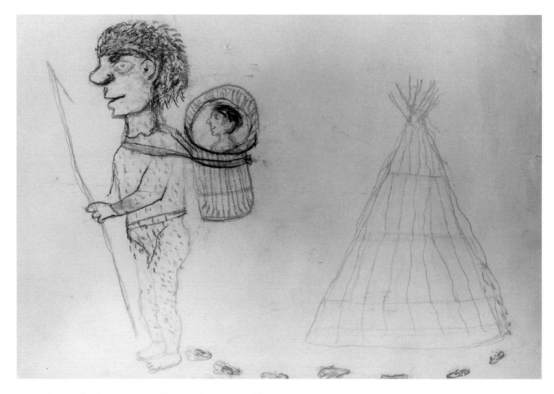

Smoke, a Shoshone storyteller on the Fort Hall reservation, drew this picture of Tsoavits, the man-eating ogre from Shoshone mythology who spirited off his victims in a basket. Many Shoshone believed that Tsoavits's basket was lined with thorns.

only weapon that could kill Tsoavits.

One story of creation related how Wolf had formed the earth after a flood covered the world. Muskrat fetched mud from the bottom of the sea, and Wolf stretched and modeled this mud into the earth. Wolf and Coyote and their wives created humans. Coyote put animals on earth when he opened the pen where Wolf had corralled them. Coyote helped people obtain fire and pine nuts and brought the Shoshone to the Great Basin in a water-carrying basket.

Wolf had created a perfect world where life was everlasting, but Coyote insisted upon a cycle of life in which humans were born, married, produced their own children, and died. This concept of life and death applied to plants and animals as well as to humans. Each living being in the Great Basin was part of the cycle of life.

The Shoshone marked important changes in life with ceremonies and rituals. Birth, puberty, marriage, and death were celebrated in ceremonies called "rites of passage," during which individuals undergoing the change of status—from youth to adulthood, for example, or from pregnancy to motherhood—were separated from society for a period, followed certain prescribed practices, and were then reincorporated in their new roles.

A Shoshone woman expecting a child, for instance, followed many ritualistic practices to assure that her child would be healthy and grow up to be a productive member of Shoshone society. She and her husband refrained from making corded rope during the pregnancy so that the baby would not be strangled by its umbilical cord as it was born. The mother ate mostly soups and abstained from fattening foods lest the baby become fat and lazy. She drank large quantities of hot water to assure an easy labor.

When it was time to give birth, the woman did so in a small lodge apart from everyone else. She was assisted by a midwife, a woman who had received knowledge of the birthing process in dreams and who knew which plants would ease labor pains. At the time of the birth, a Shoshone husband assisted his wife in many ways. He too drank hot water to afford his wife an easy labor, and he too ate light foods and avoided meat. When the baby was born, it was bathed in warm water; the father also bathed in a cold creek.

After the birth, both father and mother moved about the camp performing chores to ensure that the baby would be hardworking and contribute to the group. The mother and baby then lived apart from everyone else for one month. Finally, mother, father, and baby purified and brought blessings upon themselves by bathing and painting themselves red. They then rejoined the group.

Childhood for the Shoshone was a time of joy. Children were rarely punished by their parents for disobedience; a gentle reminder was usually all it took for a child to understand the need for cooperative behavior in the group. For they were, like adults, expected to contribute to the group's well-being.

When small, children gathered fruits and seeds with the women. At the time of communal hunts, they helped gather brush to form corrals, and their shouts helped drive rabbits and birds into nets. Girls ground pine nuts with a mano, and boys shot arrows at small game such as squirrels, which made a welcome addition to the family dinner pot. While men hunted birds, Shoshone children stalked the ground, raiding birds' nests for eggs.

But there was time for games as well. Many games taught Shoshone boys and girls the survival skills they would later need for their life in the Great Basin. Shoshone children loved hoop and pole games: using a stick to guide a hoop over the earth, they developed the ability to run great distances without tiring. Archery contests were held to see who could shoot an arrow through the quickly moving hoop. These were skills that would bring game to feed the family in a few short years. Balls of mud were used in jug-

This Shoshone woman has draped herself with ornaments made of elk teeth.

gling contests that developed quickness and dexterity. String games such as cat's cradle translated into basket making and net making as Shoshone boys and girls became men and women.

Puberty rituals represented a change from childhood to adulthood. When Shoshone boys and girls became adults, they had new responsibilities and trials to undertake. In traditional Shoshone culture, boys marked this passage by departing from the group camp to the foothills. Here, the Shoshone boy sought contact with the spirits in a vision quest. The spirits might favor him with special abilities that would allow him to become a good hunter or scout or perhaps a swift runner. These talents would allow him to contribute to the welfare of the group and eventually help support a family.

For girls, the onset of menstruation signaled their availability for marriage. As in most hunting societies, women's menstruation was deemed dangerous to men, so the girls were separated from the group and lived in a brush lodge at a distance from the camp. Here, they underwent puberty ceremonies: they abstained from eating meat, dressed in sagebrush costumes, and were symbolically cleansed with water sprinkled upon them with a wand of big sagebrush. Then the girls were given new clothes to wear, and their bodies were painted to indicate their new status. They reentered the group as marriageable women.

Because Shoshone men mostly hunted and Shoshone women mostly gathered, marriage was an essential economic institution. When many Shoshone families came together at the piñon villages, marriage partners were sought. The young men and women had time to watch and consider marriage partners during the dancing and games that followed the harvest.

The Shoshone term for the round dance was *natayati*, which means "lift-

This painting on an elk hide was done by a Shoshone man in the early 20th century. In a style common to many Native American peoples, it depicts several elements of traditional northern Shoshone culture, including a war dance (center) and buffalo hunt (surrounding).

ing feet together." The entire community joined in the dance, holding hands and moving with bent knees clockwise in a circle. The dancing was accompanied by instruments such as drums, rasps, rattles, and four-holed flutes, and everyone lent his or her voice to the singing. The round dances were performed to songs written by a *hupiakanti*, or round-dance poet, to whom the words were revealed by spirits during his dreams or vision quest. The principal singer at round dances knew many songs, often about the beauty of the Great Basin, and the verses were repeated again and again as all the Shoshone joined in.

Many games followed the harvest as well. One of the best-loved Shoshone entertainments was a guessing game, in which two teams passed four decorated sticks back and forth and team members tried to guess where each stick was. This was accompanied by singing, joking, hand motions, and swaying, all designed to confuse the opposing team. Score-keepers kept track with wooden sticks.

Both men and women had special sports. Shoshone women played a game called shinny, somewhat like field hockey, in which a braided-skin puck or ball stuffed with animal hair was propelled toward a goal with a short stick. Shoshone men had races in which they kicked a stuffed ball to a goal line.

These Shoshone men are attired for the Grass Dance, which was celebrated in the early spring to ensure plentiful food in the upcoming months. The dancers are wearing beaded vests, bandoliers, leggings, and moccasins of various design.

During these games, as well as in the dancing that took place after the piñon harvest, young men and women had the chance to impress possible mates. Parents made inquiries of other families on behalf of their sons and daughters, and then the marriage itself might be accomplished with little ceremony. After marriage, the couple most often lived with the wife's parents, with the new husband contributing his hunting skills to his new family. When the wife gave birth to their first child, the couple usually moved into their own lodging, taking with them perhaps an elder who needed food and care.

Sometimes, social adhesion was achieved by the marriage of the brothers of one family to the sisters of another. A good hunter—who had the means to feed many mouths—might even take more than one wife, possibly two sisters from the same family. A woman whose husband had died might marry his brother, and vice versa.

Traditional Shoshone belief held that at death the spirit traveled to a place of abundance—a world with rich harvests of pine nuts, grass seeds, and roots, as well as plentiful game and fish. The land of the dead was reached by following the Milky Way, which the Shoshone called "the backbone of the world."

The corpse of the deceased was painted as on festive occasions, usually with stripes of white and red, and dressed in its best clothes. Members of the family prayed that the spirit would follow the starry path to the other world and leave, rather than haunt them. The burning of big sagebrush by the Shoshone at death or when ghosts were present signified purification and protection of the living.

The corpse was then removed from its home and wrapped in a mat of buckskin. It was transported to a burial place and laid to rest with personal items from daily life: women were often buried with cooking utensils and men with hunting equipment. The grave was covered with rocks to protect the corpse from wild animals. The Shoshone mourned the departed for two or three days: to show their grief, women slashed their arms and legs with knives so that blood ran down them, and cut their hair short to ear length; men untied their braids and cut their hair to shoulder length.

The family members wore the same mourning clothes for half a year. Then they returned to the grave site, painted themselves red, and donned new clothes. A round dance was held, and mourners were urged to abandon their unhappy state and join in the dance. For the Shoshone, the circling of the dancers represented the continuing circle of life. The joining of hands showed their identity and solidarity as a group.

The Shoshone lived in this way for hundreds of years. But in the 18th century, a new element was to come to their lands. To the east lay the new United States of America, and this new nation was gradually spreading west, eventually to cross into the lands of the Shoshone. ▲

For most Americans, Sacajawea is perhaps the best known Shoshone. This young Native American woman helped guide the Lewis and Clark expedition across the western United States.

THE
LEGACY
OF
SACAJAWEA

Long before the Shoshone first saw white men, the influence and goods of white Europeans had reached the Great Basin. Spanish conquistadores, soldiers of fortune, used European technology to conquer the great Aztec empire in Mexico in 1521. They then moved north with their guns and iron tools, and they traveled in a strange new way that was to profoundly change the face of Native American culture: they came on horseback.

Native groups living in the Southwest were the first to acquire horses from the Spanish, and they in turn traded them to their northern neighbors. Horse were eagerly sought by many native groups, because, mounted on a horse, a man could quickly cover vast distances. He could surprise his enemies, carry off booty and captives, and then swiftly escape. A man on a horse could follow the great herds of buffalo and be assured of a rich haul of meat and large hides with which to construct his shelter and clothing.

By about 1700, therefore, the old forager way of life common to various Native American groups began to give way to a new life-style on the plains. Large groups banded together to form hunting societies, pitching their tipis together and becoming highly organized in their exploitation of the buffalo. East of the Rocky Mountains on the Great Plains, for example, the Sioux and Cheyenne became great nations with warriors mounted on horseback.

The Shoshone living on the edge of the Great Basin also acquired horses, and some crossed into Wyoming to become the Eastern Shoshone. One group of Eastern Shoshone then moved south to become the Comanche, the greatest warriors and hunters of the southern plains. The Northern Paiute and Shoshone in what is now southern Idaho joined together to become the Bannock Shoshone.

But the harsh environment in the interior of the Great Basin was unsuitable for horses. They needed water, which was scarce in the Great Basin, and ate wild grasses that were a major food source for the Shoshone who lived there. And the Shoshone did not need horses to harvest the piñon nuts that made up their fall and winter diet; even hunting rabbits was more efficiently done with traditional nets than on horseback.

Horses were thus useless to the traditional Shoshone way of life within the Great Basin but well suited to border areas rich in grasses and large game. The central Shoshone soon found these choice environments taken over by newly mounted neighbors. Riding on horses and armed with European guns, these groups raided Shoshone camps, capturing women and children for slaves and killing men. Without horses, the Shoshone could not pursue their enemies, and their bows and arrows were no match for firearms.

The harmony of the Great Basin had been broken. Many Shoshone retreated deeper into the interior of the Great Basin, where they would be safe from these armed and mounted raiders, and there they continued the traditional forager way of life that other Shoshone had abandoned in favor of buffalo hunting. Thus the harshness of the Great Basin

became a refuge for many of the Shoshone.

This was the world into which the Shoshone girl Sacajawea was born in 1788 or 1789, a few miles southeast of the Salmon River in the western Rocky Mountains in what is today Idaho. Sacajawea was 10 years old when she traveled with her family to the place called Three Forks in what is now Montana, between Butte and Bozeman, where three rivers join to form the headwaters of the Missouri River. Against this backdrop, the major events in Sacajawea's life and an important chapter in the early history of the United States were played out. For Sacajawea was to escort a team of white Americans along the entire length of the 2,700-mile Missouri River, making a major contribution to the history of the nation.

The saga of Sacajawea began with a raid on the Shoshone camp at Three Forks by mounted Minitari warriors armed with guns. Sacajawea was picking berries with other women and children when the raiders struck. Sacajawea had probably listened to the stories of such raids around evening campfires. Trying desperately to escape the raiders, she scrambled across a shoal in the river, but, along with another girl, she was taken captive.

Sacajawea then lived with the Minitari as a slave, learning their language but not forgetting her own. When she reached marriageable age (about 15 years old), she was either bought or won from a Minitari chief by a French-

(continued on page 53)

BEAUTY AND PRACTICALITY

The Shoshone people survived and thrived in the barren, inhospitable Great Basin through their adaptability and their extraordinary ingenuity. The tribe's watertight plant-fiber baskets are just one example of Shoshone artisans' ability to blend beauty and practicality under harsh conditions. As white encroachment on their lands sent them onto reservations with tribes such as the Sioux and Arapaho, the Shoshone adapted still further—borrowing their neighbors' innovations and adding their own design elements. Through their art, they have retained and developed their identity despite more than a century of forced acculturation.

Soft-soled moccasins with floral beadwork became popular among native groups west of the Rockies during the early reservation years. The "Shoshone Rose" motif on the top of these women's moccasins originated early in this century and is still used today.

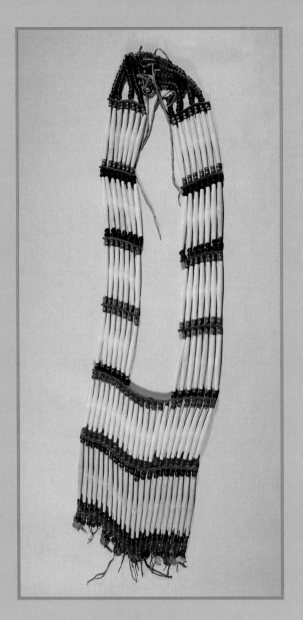

This women's breastplate is made from alternating rows of hairpipes and beads strung together on rawhide. The tapering, columnar hairpipes are so called because they were once used as hair ornaments. The Shoshone first made hairpipes from conch shells obtained through trade with West Coast tribes; later, an enterprising trader set up a New Jersey factory to make copies from bone. This style of breastplate, with its red and green cut glass beads, was popular among the Shoshone of the late 1890s.

The baby carriers of the Shoshone, Flathead, and Kutenai tribes consisted of animal skins sewed onto tapering, elongated slats that came to a rounded top. This toy carrier is scaled down to carry a little girl's doll. The flat, neat stitchery and the choice of colors on this example are characteristic of the work of Shoshone craftswomen at the turn of this century.

Eagle-feather headdresses are closely associated with Plains tribes. This Shoshone headdress was made around the turn of this century, when military native groups had all but died out. The privilege of wearing a headdress was originally reserved for revered leaders in battle: this one probably belonged to an elderly former warrior.

This large envelope-shaped parfleche is made of painted rawhide. The Shoshone and other nomadic Plains tribes usually made them in pairs to store their belongings on each side of a saddle.

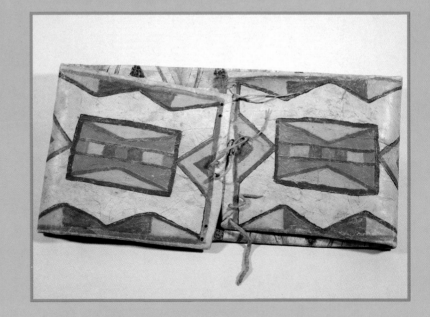

Euro-American vests were interpreted imaginatively by Native Americans. Indian men began wearing commercial cloth vests in the 1870s, and, by the end of the 19th century, Shoshone women on reservations began cutting simple leather vests and decorating them with beadwork. This example, adorned with two elk to symbolize strength and power, is typical of that period.

(continued from page 48)

This Navajo pictograph on the wall of Canyon del Muerto depicts the arrival of a Spanish expedition. The first encounter between Native Americans and the Spanish, which occurred early in the 16th century, had profound consequences for the Shoshone way of life.

Canadian interpreter named Toussaint Charbonneau. Together with another native woman he had acquired she left the Minitari to live with her new master.

Meanwhile, only a year or so before Sacajawea began living with Charbonneau, the president of the United States, Thomas Jefferson, completed the Louisiana Purchase of 1803, paying $16 million to France for all the area watered by the Missouri River and its tributaries. In a single stroke, the physical size of the United States had doubled.

After the purchase, the vast new territories needed to be explored by their new "owners." President Jefferson wanted information on the area's geography, on its mineral resources, and, above all, on the native people who were engaged in the lucrative fur trade, which was controlled by the British based in Canada.

Jefferson requested funds from Congress to survey the newly acquired lands in order to find a route to the Pacific and thus extend the external commerce of the United States. In this way, U.S. claims to the Oregon territory could also be strengthened. The dream of a nation that stretched from sea to sea was a part of the philosophy of manifest destiny. To undertake the exploration, Jefferson commissioned the Corps of

William Clark had been an officer in the U.S. Army, serving in the Indian wars on the old Northwest frontier, before being chosen as co-commander of the Corps of Discovery in 1803. He subsequently served as superintendent of Indian Affairs for the Louisiana Territory.

Discovery, led by Meriwether Lewis and William Clark. His instructions to Captain Lewis stressed how they were to behave with the native peoples they encountered: "In all ye dealings with the natives, treat them in the most friendly and conciliatory manner which their conduct will admit."

On May 14, 1804, the Corps of Discovery, led by Lewis and Clark, began their westward journey of exploration, launching their boats on the Missouri River at St. Louis against a stiff current. They had purchased firearms, scientific instruments, food, and some of the first matches ever made, and they had spent $2,000 on gifts for native peoples. Lewis and Clark understood that the success of the expedition depended upon whether they were favorably received by the people they encountered along the Missouri River and thence to the Pacific shore. They were to make careful notes on the customs and languages of all the native groups they met.

Three boats with the two captains and 43 men traveled westward on the Missouri. The expedition was well received by the people living along the river, who were especially fascinated by York, Clark's black servant, the first black person they had ever seen, and by the violin carried by a member of the expedition named Cruzat. When the party made camp, the men of the corps often danced to the violin, much to the amusement of their Indian hosts.

The boats made good progress, despite the hard paddling against the current of the Missouri. They made winter quarters near what is now Bismarck, North Dakota, where they were visited by members of the Mandan tribe. Among the guests at the camp listening to Cruzat's violin were Charbonneau and his two native women.

The captains settled in for the winter and made plans to acquire horses to carry their scientific equipment and baggage across the Rocky Mountains once the weather broke. Lewis and Clark learned from the Mandans that the group with horses living nearest to the Rocky Mountains were the Shoshone—and no one but Sacajawea could speak the Shoshone language. Lewis and Clark decided to engage Charbonneau and Sacajawea as interpreters.

That winter, Sacajawea gave birth to a child. Lewis's diaries note the hard labor she suffered: she was given rattlesnake rings to relieve her pain and hasten the birth. After consuming two rings, she gave birth to a boy who was nicknamed Pomp by Lewis. When spring arrived, Sacajawea secured the child in a carrying basket on her back and traveled westward along the Missouri River with the expedition—progressing nearer and nearer to her Shoshone homeland.

During the westward journey, Sacajawea's survival skills—learned as a child among the Shoshone—became important for the success of the corps. She collected edible roots during the spring to supplement the group's diet; she tanned hides and repaired and manufactured equipment; she cooked food and identified various tribes by their moccasin prints.

Perhaps her most famous exploit was the rescuing of valuable medicines, books, journals, and items for trade when a boat keeled over in the swift Missouri current. Lewis's journal records the mishap: "The woman, to whom I ascribe equal fortitude and resolution

Meriwether Lewis was private secretary to President Thomas Jefferson before helping lead the Corps of Discovery. Lewis's background might have suggested that he was less suited than Clark to head an expedition of exploration, but he proved no less able a commander.

with any person on board at the time of the accident, caught and preserved most of the light articles which were washed overboard." It may have been in recognition of this contribution that the captains named a branch of the Musselshell River "Birdwoman's River" in her honor. Described in Lewis's journal as "a handsome river about fifty yards wide," today the river is called Crooked Creek.

The boats had to fight the current of the Missouri, and the going was slow. The men were aware that they needed to cross the Rocky Mountains before the snows came. So when Sacajawea fell ill, their chances for obtaining horses to cross the mountains were jeopardized. In his journal Lewis wrote of his concern "for the poor object herself, then

Karl Bodmer's early 19th-century portrait of a Shoshone woman.

with a young child in her arms, [also] for the consideration of her being [their] only dependence for a friendly negotiation with the Snake [Shoshone] Indians on whom [they] depend for horses to assist [them] in [their] portage from the Missouri to the Columbia River."

Lewis treated Sacajawea with "two doses of barks and opium" as well as mineral water from a natural spring "strongly impregnated with sulphur." On June 24, 1805, he reported "the Indian woman . . . now perfectly recovered." When Sacajawea announced in late July that she recognized the country they were passing through, the party was greatly cheered. Soon, she announced, they would come to the place where three rivers joined—the spot where Sacajawea had traveled with her family each year to harvest berries and grasses, and where she had been captured as a child.

To the men of the expedition, Three Forks was "the head of the Missouri yet unknown to the civilized world." Its discovery was a triumph of the expedition. The captains christened the three rivers after the backers of the Corps of Discovery—the secretary of the treasury, the secretary of state, and the president of the United States—by calling the three rivers the Gallatin, the Monroe, and the Jefferson. The party headed west along the Jefferson, and soon Sacajawea recognized Beaverhead Rock in the distance. It was near this rock, she reported, beyond the mountains, that her people spent their summers fishing from a river that flowed west.

Lewis set off westward with an advance party to try to acquire horses. On the third day, his party reached the Continental Divide, the backbone of the North American continent. Looking west, Lewis saw high mountains partially covered with snow. "The ridge," he noted in his journals, "formed the dividing line between the waters of the Atlantic and Pacific Oceans." All the rivers to the east flowed toward the Atlantic, and those to the west toward the Pacific.

The next day, Lewis encountered two Shoshone women and a little girl, who were terrified by the sight of the stranger. But he had learned from Sacajawea that the Shoshone ceremony of painting cheeks was a sign of peace, so he painted the women's cheeks bright red, offering them beads and trinkets. The women led the party to the Shoshone encampment, where they found about 60 warriors mounted on excellent horses.

Lewis put down his gun and approached the chiefs with a flag to show his peaceful intentions. The women showed their gifts and spoke with the head chief, and soon Lewis was welcomed with a traditional embrace by the Shoshone. His journal records the event: "[We] were all so caressed and besmeared with the greasepaint that I was heartily tired of their national hug." Next, the Shoshone pulled off their moccasins, a custom, Lewis learned, that "indicated the sacred sincerity of their professions." A peace pipe was passed around with

great formality, and Lewis was led to a lodge where he was seated on green boughs and antelope skins.

He spent the next few days communicating in sign language with the head chief of the Shoshone band, Cameahwait. Lewis indicated to Cameahwait that there was a Shoshone woman with his main party who would negotiate on their behalf, and Cameahwait agreed to hear her. They returned to the main party where signs of goodwill and ceremonies were performed. After a peace pipe began to circulate among the Shoshone and corps members, Sacajawea was called in to interpret. She gave a cry of joy as she discovered that Cameahwait was none other than her brother. She told Cameahwait of the need for horses to transport the men and their equipment and provisions across the mountains.

Negotiations continued in English, French, Shoshone, and Minitari. Lewis asked the Shoshone for 30 horses and a guide, and he emphasized the friendly attitude and desire for trade on the part of the United States. The Shoshone warned the party that the river that flowed westward from Shoshone territory into the Columbia River could not be navigated and that there was no hope for a passage by water to the Pacific coast. But an old Shoshone man, called Toby by the explorers, told of a route to the north; he and his four sons then became guides for the expedition. It took two weeks of arduous travel to go north to Lolo Creek, just south of Missoula, Montana—a trip that today

Karl Bodmer's engraving and aquatint of a buffalo hunt. Europeans dramatically changed Plains and western Indian cultures when they introduced the horse. As white Americans pressed westward after Lewis and Clark's explorations, the horse would be followed by an even more dramatic innovation: the railroad.

would take about three hours by car.

By then the exploring party's supplies were exhausted, and hunting met with no success. They camped a week at a creek they christened Hungry Creek. In their desperation, the men slaughtered a horse, but Sacajawea and the other Shoshone found the idea of horse meat abhorrent and refused to eat it.

Finally, they descended the mountains west of the Rockies and reached Weippe Prairie, Idaho, where they made camp among the Nez Percé Indians. Cordially received, they feasted on salmon, buffalo meat, and camas, which made the men ill after their deprivation.

The Nez Percé chief, Twisted Hair, drew a map of three rivers on white elk skin. Today, these are called the Clearwater River, the Snake River, and the Columbia River, which flows into the Pacific Ocean. Lewis and Clark built canoes to take advantage of the currents, and the Nez Percé provided three guides to take the group down to the meeting point of the Snake and Columbia. Old Toby and his sons returned to the Shoshone camp.

Along the Snake River, the exploration party encountered many groups of Indians camped for salmon fishing. But the presence of Sacajawea, with her baby strapped to her back, reassured them that the party was peaceful, as it again reassured native groups who were terrified by the noise when Clark shot a crane and a duck along the Columbia River. As Clark noted in his journal, "[No] woman ever accompanied a war party in this quarter."

The river was punctuated by waterfalls and rapids, causing the men to portage their canoes by lowering them on ropes of braided elk skin. The Great Falls, the Short Narrows, and the Long Narrows were negotiated before the famous Great Shoot. When the fog lifted on November 7, 1805, the party glimpsed the Pacific for the first time. "O the joy!" noted Clark. "That ocean, the object of all our labors, the reward of all our anxieties. The cheering view exhilarated the spirits of all the party, who were still more delighted on hearing the distant roar of the breakers." Jefferson's dream had been achieved.

The men hoped to encounter trading vessels at the mouth of the Columbia River in order to make their homebound journey by sea. They were disappointed, however, and had to make camp for the winter before they began their overland journey back east. On the return trip, Charbonneau and Sacajawea remained with the Mandans. Clark offered to take their little son, "a beautiful, promising child," but the boy was not weaned, and the parents refused.

Charbonneau was paid for his services (although Sacajawea was not) and given a note by Clark: "This man has been very serviceable to us, and his wife was particularly useful among the Shoshones. Indeed, she has borne with a patience truly admirable the fatigues of so long a route encumbered with the charge of an infant who is even now only nineteen months old."

The territory explored by the Corps of Discovery was mapped into 10 states that were later added to the United States: Missouri, Kansas, Nebraska, Iowa, South Dakota, North Dakota, Montana, Idaho, Washington, and Oregon. Soon waves of settlers from the East would wash over the dry lands of the Great Basin, eager for the opportunities they would find in this new land. The stage had been set for a new chapter in the history of the Shoshone. ▲

Buffalo hunters blast away at a scattering herd as a train screams through. White hunters were paid sizable bounties for slain buffalo as an aid to both the construction of the railroad and the pacification of Native American populations.

THE
CIRCLE
IS
BROKEN

In the early 1800s the Shoshone often traded their baskets for obsidian and shells from other native peoples, and in 1805 they told Clark also of "the white people with whom they traded for horses mules cloth metal beads and the shells which they woar as orniment." The Spanish colonists to the south of the Great Basin had a limited but significant trading relationship with the native groups, trading along the Old Spanish Trail. What the Europeans sought from the native peoples was slaves. In return, the Europeans gave the Indians horses, arms, and trinkets such as beads, buttons, and brightly colored cloth, which were worn as status items. Bands of mounted native raiders armed with European firearms attacked their neighbors to capture women and children.

The horse, rifle, and slave trade in the southern Great Basin had painful consequences for the Shoshone. Some groups were wiped out. Others retreated farther and farther into the Great Basin. This devastating process intensified when more whites came into the territory.

The next group of white people to come to the Great Basin were the fur trappers, in the 1820s: for one of President Jefferson's objects in financing the Corps of Discovery was to help American trappers eclipse their British competitors. The British Hudson Bay Company, based in Canada, competed against the American Rocky Mountain Fur Company, based in St. Louis, the point from which the Corps of Discovery had begun its expedition.

Jedediah Smith, an employee of the Rocky Mountain Fur Company, crossed central Nevada in 1827 searching for beaver. Smith found no beaver, having missed the Humboldt River to the north. He described the native peoples he encountered as "the most miserable of the human race having nothing to subsist on (nor any clothing) except grass seeds, grasshoppers, etc."

In 1828 and 1829, Peter Skene Ogden traveled through the Great Basin for the British Hudson Bay Company. Ogden and his men were the first whites to locate the Humboldt River. They trapped the beaver to extinction and deprived the Shoshone of the furs they relied upon for their winter clothing, while Ogden's animals ate the grasses the Shoshone depended upon for food. The Shoshone called the white men *taipo* and were angry that they had destroyed their resources. It was a portent of the terrible events to come.

The trappers upset Indian trading patterns with the introduction of still more trade goods: copper pots, shining glass, iron chisels, steel knives, and metal arrowheads, all of which the Indians could use—and grow dependent upon—in their daily lives. More and more European firearms were also obtained through this trade.

When the fur trade collapsed in the 1840s, some trappers used their knowledge of the Great Basin to lead groups of explorers mapping overland routes to California. What Lewis and Clark had failed to find, these men vowed they would discover. The search for a water route to the Pacific coast was their elusive goal.

These explorers first sought the legendary Buenaventura River, which they were convinced ran through the Great Basin, emerged in the Rocky Mountains, and emptied into the Pacific. But during the 1840s, John C. Frémont, a topographical engineer with the United States Army, laid to rest the notion that such a river connected the eastern and western halves of the continent. Frémont acted as an advance scout for later settlers. He recognized the Great Basin as an area of internal drainage that had to be crossed by land to reach California.

Frémont's reports established the popular image of the Great Basin in the minds of migrating Americans. He was known as the "Great Pathfinder," and his goal was to find the quickest route through the seemingly worthless lands of the Great Basin. Frémont's description of the indigenous population was as negative as his appraisal of their land. Forager groups such as the Shoshone, whose "sole employment is to obtain food," were considered by Frémont "the nearest approach to the mere animal creation."

The migrants saw little to recommend the lands of the Great Basin as suitable for settlement: the lands were no good for livestock or European crops such as wheat, barley, and rye, which depended upon an abundant and constant supply of water. Ironically, however, while scorning the Great Basin, the white migrants themselves devastated much of the fragile environment upon which the Shoshone depended for their livelihood. As the settlers passed through the Great Basin, their grazing livestock depleted the grass that grew beside the rivers and churned up the soil, leaving behind a hard turf. Diseases from the livestock devastated

Mormon wagons make their way west along the so-called Mormon Trail, which veered southwest to Utah from the Oregon Trail near the headwaters of the Sweetwater River.

populations of rabbits that supplied the Shoshone with furs and meat. And the migrants hunted larger game from wagon trains with efficient rifles, whose violent noise drove other game away.

In 1843, Charles Preuss, a mapmaker for Frémont, noted the predicament of the Northern Shoshone: "The white people have ruined the country of the Snake [Shoshone] Indians and should therefore treat them well. Almost all the natives are now obliged to live on roots, game can scarcely be seen anymore." Some Shoshone responded to this threat on their livelihood by making raids on migrant livestock and by taking the goods the migrants left when the call to lighten the load was given. The migrants defended their livestock with bullets, so Shoshone men, seeking meat to feed their families, were felled by the settlers' guns.

In 1847, a group of whites came to the Great Basin seeking refuge from their fellow whites. This group was the Mormons, members of the Church of Jesus Christ of Latter-Day Saints. The Saints, as they called themselves, believed in a doctrine revealed to their founder, Joseph Smith, on golden tablets called the Book of Mormon. Their belief in polygamy and a well-organized economic base had engendered hostility from their neighbors, which had led to the murder of Smith in 1846. Their new leader, Brigham Young, led them to the Great Basin to establish a new, self-sustaining Mormon community.

Seeing the lands of the Salt Lake valley stretched before him, Brigham Young declared in 1847, "This is the place." For these people, the Great Basin was attractive because it was in a remote area devoid of permanent settlements, where they hoped to find religious freedom and peace; they hoped that by settling in what they considered to be a no-man's-land between feuding Shoshone and Ute groups they would avoid provoking hostilities.

The tide of history was to turn the very next year. In 1848, the Treaty of Guadalupe Hidalgo concluded the Mexican-American War, and the territory of the Great Basin was acquired by the United States. That same year, the discovery of gold in California brought hopeful hordes of men with mining picks in their hands and dreams of riches in their hearts across the Great Basin. In 1849 alone, as many as 25,000 gold seekers bound for California used overland routes that crossed the Great Basin.

Some of these men followed the Oregon Trail through the South Pass, then turned southwest, crossing the Great Basin through Utah and Nevada to California. Many others took the trail established in 1833 by Joseph Reddeford Walker. A beaver trapper, Walker had gone from the Great Salt Lake to the Humboldt River. He followed the stream to its sink and crossed

This photograph of the construction of the Transcontinental Railroad was taken near the Green River in Wyoming in the winter of 1867/68. For the Native Americans of the West, the railroad may have been the single most destructive element of white settlement.

the desert, continuing across the Sierra Nevada to California. His route became known as the California Trail. Prospectors traveling through the Great Basin on the California Trail found it convenient to stop and buy supplies from the Mormons, whose colonization of Utah Territory cut across the basin, following the Humboldt River to the south. As Mormon settlements advanced to the south, some migrants took the Old Spanish Trail.

In 1848, Brigham Young was appointed superintendent of Indian affairs for the Utah Territory, which included what is today Utah and Nevada, as well as western Colorado. Young was determined that the Mormons would coexist peacefully with their native neighbors, and he formulated toward the Great Basin native peoples what has been described as the "easier-to-feed-than-fight" policy. "We always consider it cheaper to feed and clothe the Indians than to fight them," he said, "and so long as we can get access to them to feed them &c. we have no trouble with them; but when they get out of the settlements into the mountains there is danger of depredations &c. by them." Protective benevolence, education, and, ultimately, conversion to the Mormon faith were the initial elements of Young's Indian policy.

In 1854, the first Mormon mission was established. The Mormons attempted to create permanent settlements for the Shoshone, teach them agriculture, and provide them with food and clothing. But white non-Mormons, or

Gentiles, as the Mormons called them, viewed Mormon Indian policy with distrust. Believing that the Mormons wished to prevent other whites from settling in the area, they suspected the Mormons of supplying arms to the native bands who attacked migrant trains.

In 1857, members of a migrant wagon train bound for California were slaughtered by a group of fanatical Mormons as their party crossed Utah Territory. Native bands then stripped the corpses, and Mormon families took in the surviving children. The infamous Mountain Meadows Massacre, as it was called, was viewed as proof that the Mormons wished to use their influence over the native inhabitants to establish their own nation of Deseret in Utah Territory.

The following year, federal troops came to Utah by order of President James Buchanan. The troops brought the Mormons to heel and limited their control of the Utah Territory. Brigham Young was removed as governor and superintendent of Indian affairs. The troops also curtailed the guerrilla attacks by native bands on federal supply trains and California-bound wagon trains. To reinforce the presence of the United States government, Camp Floyd was established 40 miles west of Salt Lake City.

But traffic through the territory again accelerated with the discovery of the Comstock Lode in western Nevada, which sent a virtual stampede of prospectors through the Great Basin.

This had repercussions throughout the region, as the land was stripped of natural resources in order to extract the silver ore—in great demand since the outbreak of the Civil War in 1861. Mail routes, the stagecoach system, the pony express, and the telegraph line also cut through Shoshone territory—all part of the Union war effort, and all destroying vital Shoshone resources.

The great silver boom ran on wood: the opening of a mine required timbers for shoring up shafts; cordwood was needed by the miners for heating and cooking; housing for miners was constructed of lumber; and charcoal was required for smelting ore. *Carbonari*, European charcoal makers, were brought over from Italy and Switzerland to manufacture charcoal by burning wood in airtight kilns, a process that produced an extremely efficient fuel that burned hotter than wood and produced far less waste.

One central mining town in the Great Basin—Eureka, Nevada—resembled an industrial town in the Pennsylvania coal region and was dubbed "the Pittsburgh of the West." In 1873, there were 13 smelters and 600 carbonari in the town. Each day, 595 tons of ore were processed, each ton requiring 30 bushels of charcoal, amounting to a daily charcoal consumption of 17,850 bushels. A judge named Goodwin, in an official document for the state legislature, described Eureka as "a smelting camp over which rolled black clouds of dense smoke from the furnaces scented with fumes of lead and arsenic which deposited soot and black dusk."

When mining began in 1859 at the Comstock Lode, the mountains around Virginia City were covered with piñon and juniper. By 1868, there were 24 sawmills in Nevada producing 180,000 board feet of lumber daily. It has been said that Virginia City had as much wood underground as Chicago had on the surface.

Thus the environment of the Great Basin, which had scarcely changed for some 5,000 years, was dramatically altered in the late 19th century. Not only did the felling of piñon trees deprive the Shoshone of pine nuts, but the cutting of the trees themselves was considered an act of sacrilege against the sacred spirits of the trees. But little help was forthcoming from Washington, D. C. The newly appointed superintendent of Indian affairs for the Utah Territory, James Duane Doty, described the plight of the Shoshone and other groups in a letter to Washington in 1862: "The Indians have been, in great numbers, in a starving and destitute condition. No provisions having been made for them."

The miners were not alone in altering the environment, however: they created a sizable market for provisions, and this brought farmers and ranchers into the region. Ranchers' herds stripped the land of grasses, in whose place grew sagebrush and non-native weeds. Settlers, who now imposed a European style of agriculture on the Great Basin, wreaked havoc on the land. Bottomlands were plowed for crops or

A Shoshone warrior, said to be a member of Pocatello's band. For whites, Pocatello's band were the most notoriously militant Shoshone opponents of white settlement.

converted to permanent pastures for livestock. Small mammals such as rabbits fed upon the farmers' new crops, while birds pecked the seeds they sowed in the earth. These animals were considered competitors by the farmers, who resorted to traps, rifles, and poison to protect their fields.

Forage for livestock had to come from lands not under cultivation. This

Tipis of the Eastern Shoshone group led by Washakie, who was one of the first Shoshone leaders to recognize the futility of further resistance to white settlement and request a reservation for his people.

required driving flocks out to pasture and returning them to the settlements at night to protect them from predators or, more often than not, from hungry native peoples. Thousands of animal hooves turned foothills that had formerly been fertile land into dust.

Fires that the Shoshone set to favor the growth of certain herbs were blocked by the construction of trails and roads throughout the foothills. Alien plants altered the natural cover of the region and introduced new species of animals that pushed out native species. The German carp, introduced by the settlers, stripped the waterways of plants upon which waterfowl depend-

ed. The bighorn sheep and game were driven from the area or hunted by the miners for food. Overfishing, damming, and silting of local streams deprived the Shoshone of fish resources as well.

With their environment and its vital resources destroyed, many Shoshone were forced to either work at wage labor for whites, or starve. Desperate, they joined in the destruction of their own environment by taking on jobs in farming and lumbering. Captain Sam, a Shoshone chief, explained the plight of his people to federal Indian agent Sheen in about 1870. Sheen wrote that

> the game were all gone; the trees that bore pine-nuts were put down

and burned in the quartz-mills and other places; the grass-seeds, heretofore used by them for food, were no more; the grass-land all claimed by and cultivated by the white people; and . . . [the] Indians would soon be compelled to work for the ranches for two bits a day or starve.

Thus, in less than 50 years since the Shoshone had first helped Lewis and Clark find a route to the Pacific, they had lost substantial portions of their subsistence base and could no longer rely upon their traditional means of survival. Even the animals of the region found their habitat destroyed and could not survive in the altered landscape.

As larger amounts of land were taken over, small groups of Shoshone were forced to live with other Shoshone on smaller areas. This changed their relatively loose social structure and the balance of power in the Great Basin, and these changes were reinforced by Euro-American concepts about Native American nations and chiefs. The office of chief had never been a feature of traditional Shoshone culture, yet the federal agents would negotiate only with "chiefs," who made agreements on behalf of their people and received gifts in return.

The Shoshone responded to these forced changes in a variety of ways. Some were swept up in Euro-American society, with men finding work as ranch hands or in lumberyards, and women becoming domestic servants. Other Shoshone retreated still farther into lands that the white Americans had not penetrated. The Eastern Shoshone under Chief Washakie, for their part, were receptive to overtures of peace by federal Indian agents: in 1858, Washakie requested a reservation for his people. Still other Shoshone responded by raiding miners and settlers to obtain food.

Tensions between whites and native groups of the Great Basin intensified, fueled by the indiscriminate shooting of the native population by migrants passing through the Great Basin and the continued devastation of the habitat. Exaggerated accounts of Indian raids began to circulate. In one 1861 account, the Northern Shoshone chief Pocatello was said to be responsible for a massacre of 300 migrants in 60 wagons at Almo, Idaho.

Colonel Patrick Edward Connor came in 1863 with a group of California volunteers to keep the Great Basin natives (as well as the Mormons) in check, and, in retaliation for an attack attributed to Pocatello, Connor led federal troops against the Shoshone. In the Battle of Bear River, 250 Shoshone men, women, and children were killed when troops launched an attack on their camp.

Eventually, however, the mines failed. The region's new economy crumbled, and the Shoshone were left without their wage jobs. The Shoshone were forced to return to their traditional way of life, a way of life that was no longer possible because of the devastation of the Great Basin's natural resources. ▲

Chief Washakie in old age on the Wind River Reservation. Even in defeat, the Shoshone were generous: Washakie allowed his defeated Sioux and Arapaho enemies to share the reservation with his people, explaining that "they would not hurt the land by living on it."

DESPAIR
AND
HOPE

B etween 1839 and 1868, the lands of the Great Basin were organized into territories. Within each territory, the federal government assumed the task of regulating relations with the local native populations. Officially, Indian policy was based on the premise that people from these cultures could be insulated from settlers, miners, and entrepreneurs by the establishment of reservations on or near their aboriginal territory. Here, the government reasoned, Native Americans could acquire farming and livestock skills that would allow them to be self-sufficient.

There was a great difference between stated federal policy and the realities of Indian-white relations during this time. The actual practice was that local Indian populations were, at best, considered a hindrance to the development of the Great Basin. At worst, they were seen as a threat to the safety of the white population, which

now had a firm foothold in the area. Their containment on reservations would free up land for settlement and mining and protect the white population from their supposed hostile intentions.

In establishing an Indian policy, the government first had Indian agents identify various Indian groups. The agents reported to the Bureau of Indian Affairs in Washington, D.C. The absence of strict guidelines gave these federal Indian agents tremendous leeway in their actions. Furthermore, these men had vastly different backgrounds and motivations. The result was that early federal policy toward Native Americans in the Great Basin varied considerably with each agent.

Between 1852 and 1904, federal agents negotiated almost two dozen treaties with the Shoshone. Yet each time the federal government signed a treaty, local interest groups began to modify its provisions to their own advantage. In the text of the Treaty of Bridger of 1863, for example, a clerk misspelled the Kamas Prairie as the Kansas Prairie. Settlers in Idaho subsequently refused the Northern Shoshone and Bannocks access to the prairie, denying them the important camas resource. The Treaty of Ruby Valley concluded with the Western Shoshone was simply ignored by local ranching and mining interests in Nevada.

Each group of Shoshone negotiated separate treaties with the federal government, and each received different treatment. This treatment depended upon the area of the group's traditional territory, the Shoshone leadership of each group, and the attitude of the individual federal agents. The Shoshone way of life varied considerably, from foraging to hunting buffalo, and this variance also affected how Shoshone groups fared during this period. The presence or absence of resources that the white settlers found desirable, furthermore, was an important factor in all negotiations with the Shoshone.

Chief Washakie of the Eastern Shoshone had requested a reservation as early as 1858, asking for the valley of Henry's Fork for his people. The reservation was not established, however, and in 1867/68 the Union Pacific Railroad cut through traditional Eastern Shoshone territory. As the railroad was built, it brought workers and boomtowns with it. In 1867, Washakie again requested a reservation, this time in the Wind River valley, and the 1868 Treaty of Fort Bridger set aside these lands for the Eastern Shoshone. But in 1872, Washakie had to sign away part of this area, which, due to a surveying error had included many previously homesteaded ranches. For $25,000, the Eastern Shoshone released their claims on this land.

The Eastern Shoshone were a mounted plains-culture group. In 1876, Eastern Shoshone warriors assisted General George Cook in his Sioux campaign. In 1878, they supplied scouts to hunt down Bannocks in the Bannock War. When Northern Arapaho refused to be relocated to a reservation in Oklahoma, the government sent them to the lands of the Eastern Shoshone. The Northern Arapaho were provided with a military escort to the Wind River Reservation to settle next to their old Eastern Shoshone enemies. The Eastern Shoshone understood the situation to be temporary, but in reality the Arapaho were given about half the reservation.

The Northern Shoshone fared even worse than their eastern cousins. Settlers along the Boise and Braneau rivers pushed the Northern Shoshone and Bannock bands from their area. During the winter of 1867, more than 400 Indians from these bands were forced to depend on rations supplied by territory officials. That same year, the Fort Hall Reservation was established in Idaho.

Inadequate facilities and further encroachment by settlers caused even more difficulties for the groups that were relocated to the Fort Hall Reservation.

A young Shoshone man known as Pat Tyhee before (left) and after he cut his hair and adopted white man's clothing as an outward demonstration of his embrace of Christianity.

Homesteaders had settled illegally on the reservation, and the town of Pocatello was firmly established on reservation territory.

The intense hostility between settlers and Shoshone in the area barred the Shoshone from access to the traditional hunting, gathering, and fishing grounds that the federal government had guaranteed them by treaty. Hostile settlers attacked groups of Shoshone gathering food, so they were afraid to leave the reservations to forage, particularly with women and children. Fort Hall Reservation had been established as a farming reservation by the federal government, but no adequate supply of seeds and tools was provided. Plagues of insects and inadequate rations brought these Shoshone to the point of starvation.

This photograph of young Shoshone women students at the Presbyterian mission school on the Fort Hall Reservation illustrates why many Native Americans believed such educational institutions operated as agents of forcible acculturation.

The Western Shoshone Indian agent had recommended in 1859 that the government establish a reservation in Ruby Valley, Nevada, but this had never happened. In 1873, some Western Shoshone established a farm north of Palisade. This became known as the Carlin Farms in 1877, when 52 acres were set aside for use by Western Shoshone. But two settlers claimed that they had previously filed for homesteads on the land. In 1879, the land was restored to the public domain.

In 1877, the government established the Duck Valley Reservation in Nevada for those Western Shoshone not engaged at Carlin Farms. The Duck Valley Reservation was well outside the traditional territory of the Western Shoshone, so many groups refused to move to the area. By 1879, only about one in four Western Shoshone had made the move. In 1882, more than two-thirds of those Western Shoshone who had moved to the Duck Valley Reservation abandoned it: the reservation had a corrupt agent;

the government had failed to deliver promised rations; the price of supplies was high; and the price paid for crops grown on the reservation was low.

The Western Shoshone scattered back to the heart of their traditional territory, to mining districts in north-central Nevada and to Fort Hall. By 1884, only 300 people remained on the Duck Valley Reservation. The government enlarged the reservation and relocated Paiutes there. Only one-tenth of the Western Shoshone maintained residence in Duck Valley Reservation. The remaining Western Shoshone developed a life-style that combined traditional Great Basin foraging with Euro-American wage work. They signed up for seasonal work in mines or on farms and pursued their traditional way of life the rest of the time.

So unsuccessful was the government's Indian policy that fewer than 60 percent of all Great Basin native peoples were actually living on designated reservations. In 1869, the country elected Civil War general Ulysses S. Grant as president. Grant's administration attempted to apply a uniform policy to all reservations. The aim of the new policy was different from its predecessors: all native peoples of the United States were now to abandon their traditional ways of life; become workers and farmers; convert to Christianity; and become literate in the English language. Once the native peoples were "unfettered" by their own cultures, the policy makers reasoned, there would be rural American towns with populations of "acculturated Indians."

In order to accomplish these goals, all native people were to be removed to designated reservations, or new reservations would be created to contain them. This was called the Pan-Reservation Policy. The administration would put a federal agent in place in each reservation. Christian missions would be established in each community. Farming tools would be provided, and farmers themselves were to be dispatched to advise the native population at every reservation. A medical clinic, an agency with an all-white support staff, an all-Indian police force under the direction of the Bureau of Indian Affairs, and a "Court of Indian Offenses" were also to be established on every reservation.

The government began to negotiate contracts with Christian missionaries to provide personnel for the reservations and establish churches and schools. Often, young children were sent far away to boarding schools run like military academies; the idea was that if children were separated from their families at a young age, they would lose their native language, "superstitions," and "pagan practices" and return to their reservations like young Euro-Americans. The churches likewise banned native religious ceremonies and doctoring by shamans on the reservations; it forbade young Shoshone men from going on vision quests; even the dead could no longer be mourned and buried in traditional ceremonies.

Government attempts to turn Indians into farmers on all reservations, regardless of their location, met with varied success. Some reservations lacked water, and others had water usurped by white settlers living upstream. Even if the reservation population succeeded in growing crops, they had to depend upon the agent and his staff to provide farm equipment and seeds and to transport their crops to market, for agents controlled all the reservation finances. These conditions made the Shoshone and other groups dependent upon the agents at the reservations, where legal and cultural parity with whites was impossible.

The government operated on the assumption that a capitalist system, in which people accumulate wealth and fix a monetary value to all goods and services, was shared by the Shoshone and other Native American groups. But these concepts were alien to the Great Basin culture. They violated the traditional system of ethics based on harmony and social relationships.

In 1887, the government instituted the Dawes Severalty Act to promote private Native American ownership of farmland, and reservations were cut into parcels and distributed to individual farmers. This allotment policy called for land to be held in trust for the native population for 25 years. At the end of this period, the land became private property and could be sold if the local Indian agent certified that the person who held the allotment was sufficiently "civilized."

The allotment policy was disastrous for every Great Basin native group. Individuals were restricted to farming plots of land that were too small to support them adequately, while plots of desirable land were taken by whites. Starvation, disease, and despair settled over the native population of the Great Basin. When the allotment period came to an end in 1930, it was clear that government Indian policy had failed again: despite the damage done to them, the Shoshone and other Great Basin groups had nevertheless succeeded in keeping their identities intact.

During the hard times, the native peoples of the Great Basin sought help from a quarter uncontaminated by white American values and policies: the spiritual realm. Religious movements promising a better world arose, among them, the Ghost Dance, the Bear Dance, and the Sun Dance. The Ghost Dance first appeared in the Great Basin in the 1860s. In a vision, a Northern Paiute named Wodzibob was taught the Ghost Dance in which men, women, and children joined hands in a circle and sang sacred songs. Participants in the dance were to receive visions that would show them how to restore the resources upon which they had lived before the coming of the white people. Those who had died would come back to life and a new, happy existence.

In 1869, the message of the Ghost Dance swept through the Great Basin and was eagerly taken up by those who had suffered the disastrous effects of government policies and white encroachment. The Shoshone at the Fort Hall and Wind River reservations and other sites danced the Ghost Dance,

The old overtaken by the new: a Shoshone family on the Fort Hall Reservation in May 1909.

which incorporated traditional Shoshone beliefs in visions and the practice of round dancing.

In 1889, a Northern Paiute named Wovoka received a new Ghost Dance vision. The ideology of this new Ghost Dance was to live in peace with the whites. If the people would perform the Ghost Dance, live together in friendship, avoid war, and work hard, they would be reunited with friends in the other world. This new Ghost Dance was a call to strengthen the native community living within the white-dominated world. Individual redemption and change in each Ghost Dancer would ultimately bring about a new social order. The beleaguered Shoshone at Fort Hall quickly became ardent proselytizers of the Ghost Dance throughout the Great Basin. Soon, however, many groups became disillusioned with the movement. They sought a more immediate solution to the daily problems they faced.

By the 1880s, they also looked to the Bear Dance. This was performed over 10 days in late winter and was danced

The magnitude of all the losses her people had suffered is evident in the eyes of Mary Washakie, daughter of the great chief of the Eastern Shoshone, in this photograph taken on the Wind River Reservation in 1913.

to an orchestra of musical rasps. The Bear Dance emphasized reverence for the dead and spiritual healing and was believed to bring good health and camaraderie to the living during the oppressive conditions of the period. The Bear Dance was performed in the Great Basin until the 1940s.

The Sun Dance was originally a Plains Indians ceremony intended to ensure successful buffalo hunts and warfare, but it later became directed toward illness and community misery; after the 1880s it was performed to nourish the public good. In the traditional Sun Dance, a corral of 12 poles was built around a central pole with a buffalo head fixed to it and topped by an eagle. Singing and drumming accompanied men who danced to and from the central pole for three days and nights, actually attached to the pole by means of leather thongs piercing the skin of their chests. The participants danced without water, enduring pain and hardship as they sought visions that would benefit the community; their dancing was thought to produce power to cure the sick. The Sun Dance movement was thus redemptive, stressing the welfare of the community over that of individuals.

The Ghost Dance, Bear Dance, and Sun Dance all grew in response to the oppressive conditions of the time and the loss of traditional avenues of contact with the spiritual world. These activities were attempts by the Shoshone and other native peoples to preserve their unique cultural identities. Furthermore, during the 1860s and 1870s, the traditional Shoshone round dance, although accommodating the restrictions of the reservation system, developed in ways that helped further Shoshone identity. It became known as the *fandango*, a Spanish word meaning celebration or dance. The fandango differed from the traditional round dance in ways that represented the Shoshone response to changes in their own socioeconomic conditions, as well as their changing relationship with other Native Americans and white Americans.

The fandangos were performed on a larger scale than traditional round dances, reflecting the fact that the Shoshone were no longer scattered across the Great Basin but were now concentrated in larger groups. The Shoshone took advantage of the large numbers gathering as a unique survival tool: in 1867, for example, the Shoshone sponsored a fandango in order to assemble a large number of people and petition the federal government for relief during a particularly hard winter. In response to the challenges of white American culture, fandangos came to be held in conjunction with holidays such as the Fourth of July. Fandangos were also used to solve differences with other native groups, particularly the Northern Paiutes, who moved into traditional Shoshone territory from the west, seeking jobs in mining and ranching.

Just as the Shoshone created their way of life by adapting to the harsh landscape of the Great Basin, they also prevailed in preserving elements of their culture in the face of difficult conditions imposed during this dark period of their history. There was little loss of native languages despite the fact that children had been forbidden to speak them in school. New reservation-based social and political groups emerged. As pressure from white groups increased, Shoshone alienation from white society grew stronger. The result was a keen sense of separateness from white American society and a fierce pride in their culture. ▲

Entitled Used and Abused, *this pencil-and-ink drawing by contemporary Western Shoshone artist Jack Malotte delineates some of the issues affecting the tribe today. Foremost among them, as so often in the tribe's history, is land use, as defense contractors and mining and electrical power companies become increasingly interested in the natural resources of the Shoshone land holdings.*

MENDING
THE
CIRCLE

When Franklin Delano Roosevelt was elected president in 1933, the United States was at the height of the Great Depression. To combat the depression, the Roosevelt administration set up reform legislation and made vast expenditures of public money to develop natural resources and offer work to the millions of unemployed. This was called the New Deal.

There was an Indian New Deal as well. President Roosevelt appointed John Collier as Commissioner of Indian Affairs, and Collier worked hard to reverse some of the consequences of past federal Indian policy. The Indian New Deal promised the Shoshone and other native groups improved land, better health care, and greater cultural and political freedom.

Commissioner Collier halted the allotment of land and restored former reservation land to tribal ownership. Tribes were allowed to consolidate their

lands and purchase more to restore an adequate base. Reservations were created for native peoples who had none.

Federal programs provided improved health care, employment, and community development, and offered college scholarships to young Native American students.

While improving economic conditions, Collier sought to reinvigorate Native Americans' sense of tribal community and culture. Bans on native religious and ceremonial activities were lifted; native customs and traditions were sanctioned once again. Native art and traditional crafts such as basketry, pottery, leatherwork, and beadwork were encouraged.

And the Tribal Reorganization Act of 1934 provided the principles of self-government. This would be achieved through elected tribal councils and chairmen, so the Shoshone and other groups would no longer be subject to the arbitrary and paternalistic rule of federal Indian agents.

Many Shoshone were skeptical of the government's intentions. With the death of Washakie and other chiefs, the Shoshone lacked men who could fill a leadership role. Furthermore, reservation life had deprived the Shoshone of traditional paths to leadership, such as prowess in hunting or warfare. Nevertheless, from 1936 to 1980, most Great Basin native groups were incorporated in some sort of tribal council system.

Capital for farming and ranching ventures was provided by the government. At Duck Valley, Fort Hall, and Wind River, sheep-raising cooperatives were formed. Cattlemen's associations were established, and the land at Duck Valley was irrigated by constructing a reservoir. Credit unions under Bureau of Indian Affairs management provided funds. New Deal programs for the general population such as the Work Projects Administration brought some jobs, as did the Indian Civilian Conservation Corps.

The Indian New Deal began to achieve results. Improved healthcare resulted in a decline of tuberculosis and other diseases that had taken a deadly toll on the Shoshone since the coming of Euro-Americans to the Great Basin. Infant mortality was reduced, and the Shoshone population began to increase as the rate of births outstripped the rate of deaths for the first time in decades.

But World War II cut short many promises made by the Indian New Deal:

funds were diverted to the war effort, and when programs were curtailed, jobs disappeared. By 1943, the Indian office headquarters had moved to Chicago and had little influence in Washington. The end of World War II saw yet another reversal of federal Indian policy. Federal trust responsibilities were to be eliminated, and reservations would be abolished. In short, the government was getting out of the "Indian business." The special status that had protected the land on Indian reservations was to be withdrawn in a policy known as termination.

This termination legislation was strongly supported by Senator Patrick McCarran from Nevada and Senator Arthur B. Watkins from Utah, whose states contained a large portion of traditional Shoshone territory. But the Shoshone and other Great Basin native groups fought this new policy and, when asked to draw up termination plans, refused to do so.

The senators supported the establishment of a U.S. Claims Commission in 1946, which was to offer monetary compensation to native groups to aid in the termination process. It was agreed in Congress that the United States should pay "just debts" to native peoples as a way of rectifying past misdeeds. Further, the settlement of claims would encourage the "progress of the Indians who desire to be rehabilitated at the white man's level in the white man's economy." Finally, the settlement of claims would allow "proper development of the public domain."

Western Shoshone and Northern Paiute women assemble electronics equipment on the Duck Valley Reservation in Nevada in the early 1970s. This was one of several industrial-development and vocational-training programs that have been introduced, with varying degrees of success, on Shoshone reservations.

Shoshone women play shinny, a traditional game that combines elements of hockey, soccer, and lacrosse.

Native groups were given five years to file petitions. During hearings on Shoshone petitions, the commission used maps drawn by Superintendent James D. Doty for treaties negotiated with the Northern, Western, and Eastern Shoshone during the summer and fall of 1863. Doty had drawn the boundaries of the territories occupied by all of the Northern Shoshone, Western Shoshone, and part of the Eastern Shoshone in red ink. Each Shoshone "chief" had signed the treaties with an *X*, and the treaties had been transmitted to the Senate for ratifi-

cation and been signed by President Abraham Lincoln in 1864.

Anthropologists served as witnesses for the Shoshone and many other native groups. Robert F. and Yolanda Murphy prepared an ethnohistorical report to present to the commission, in which they explained the traditional Great Basin life-style and asserted that Shoshone territorial distribution differed from Doty's 1863 maps. This testimony was particularly significant in the case of the Western Shoshone. The government had initially argued that the Western Shoshone were "scattered over several communities" and did not constitute a "recognized tribe." The Western Shoshone finally won recognition as a coherent group and petitioned the commission.

Compensation by the commission to Great Basin groups totaled $137,206,129. Included in this figure is $26,145,189 that was rejected by the Western Shoshone as fair compensation for their traditional territory. Once the award was made, the petitioning group disposed "of all rights, claims, or demands which said petitioners . . . could have asserted with respect to said tract . . . and said petitioners . . . [were] barred thereby from asserting any rights, claims, or demands against" the U.S. government in the future.

Another aspect of the new federal Indian legislation was the institution of mineral leasing by non-natives. Coal, oil, gas, uranium, phosphates, and other nonrenewable natural resources are found in abundance in the territory of the Shoshone and other Great Basin native groups. Large leases were negotiated for oil and gas at Wind River and for phosphates at Fort Hall. In 1956, Wind River earned $1.3 million from mineral leasing. This figure increased steadily over the next two decades so that oil and gas royalties provided the major source of income for the reservation. Fort Hall received only $150,000 from mineral leases in 1967.

Legislative efforts at termination were also affected by returning Shoshone veterans who had served in World War II. These men had been guaranteed apartments, job training, and employment in cities under the Bureau of Indian Affairs relocation program. But they were frustrated by the discrimination and layoffs they had experienced in the white world. By the late 1950s, they were returning home to the Fort Hall and Wind River reservations.

In the 1950s, jurisdiction over Indian policy from the federal government transferred to state governments. Legislation was passed to hasten the termination of tribes by encouraging the physical relocation of native peoples and ensuring their integration into the mainstream of American society.

Shoshone veterans sought alternatives for their reservations, as termination was not an alternative they would consider. From their ranks emerged a new generation of Shoshone leaders. During the 1960s, this new generation of Great Basin native leaders was instrumental in the rejection of federal termination policy.

President Lyndon B. Johnson's Great Society program of the 1960s included social and economic policies that promoted yet another government Indian policy, self-determination. The Indian Self-Determination Act of 1975 was designed to provide for tribal decision-making mechanisms and control of local policies. The federal government assumed a protective role while increasing tribal participation in government policies.

The Council of Energy Resource Tribes (CERT) was formed in 1976 in order to help Indians negotiate from a stronger position with multinational corporations and reduce their dependency on the Bureau of Indian Affairs for financial management and technical advice. Wind River Shoshone and Fort Hall Northern Shoshone and Bannock joined the organization to help administer their mineral resources. Despite the help of CERT and the large amounts of revenue generated by mineral leasing, Wind River Reservation has been negatively affected by the illegal diversion of their resources by private companies.

Another economic development affecting the resources of the Great Basin occurred after World War II, when there was a rise in red-meat consumption by Americans. Woodland was viewed as potential pasture for cattle grazing, so the Forest Service carved up national forest woodlands with bulldozers and chains in order to create pasture. Chaining was a new and efficient way of uprooting trees, in which two ends of a battleship anchor were attached to two crawler tractors, which were then driven parallel to each other; the dragging chain and anchor uprooted the trees in their path. After the trees were piled, the area was seeded with forage plants such as crested wheat grass, a plant native to central Asia. Burning, herbicide spraying, and the felling of large trees were used to completely strip the land of its tree cover. From 1960 to 1972, over a third of a million acres of piñon and juniper woodlands were chained by the Forest Service and the Bureau of Land Management in Utah and Nevada alone.

There was no nationwide environmental protection movement at this time. Except for the protests of the Shoshone and other Great Basin groups who deplored the despoliation of their sacred piñon trees, the practice went unheeded. Ironically, the effects of this practice were quickly counteracted by piñon jays that planted piñon seeds and thrushes that defecated them But it takes 75 years for a piñon tree to reach maturity. Some of the fallen piñon trees were several hundred years old; their piñon nuts had nourished generations of Shoshone during the harsh Great Basin winters.

Out-of-state commercial nut dealers were given exclusive harvesting permits in many remaining piñon tree areas, and Shoshone who wished to harvest piñon nuts were charged a hefty fee. The sulfur dioxide waste from coal-fired power plants generating electric energy for metropolitan areas did further damage to piñon and juniper woodlands, and permanent damage was inflicted as well upon irreplaceable Great Basin native archaeological sites, allegedly protected under the Antiquities Act of 1906. Their full-scale destruction occurred at the hands of the very agency charged with their protection.

The desecration of the land led to the radicalization of many Great Basin groups, in particular the Western Shoshone. They were outraged at the felling of trees, at their lack of access to traditional resources guaranteed in treaties with the U.S. government, and

"Hard to Be Traditional When You're All Plugged In," by Shoshone Jack Malotte.

at the wholesale destruction of their cultural heritage.

In 1972, the American Indian Movement (AIM) organized a demonstration in the nation's capital, a demonstration known as the Trail of Broken Treaties. To attract national attention, AIM participants arrived the week of the presidential elections but were refused meetings with officials.

During the 1980s, the trend to transfer Indian affairs to state jurisdiction began again. Many states, particularly

Nevada and Utah, have long sought stronger control over natural resources found in traditional Shoshone territory. But the voices of the Shoshone and other Great Basin peoples have become stronger in their struggle to preserve their cultural identity and natural resources.

Formerly, elders had preserved the oral traditions that offered a unique Shoshone point of view. But the voices of the elders were dying out. Without resources and largely nonliterate, gener-

Dressed in traditional ceremonial garb, a Shoshone dancer examines the wares at a crafts booth during the annual Native American festival held by the Te-Moak tribe of Western Shoshone in Elko, Nevada.

ations of Shoshone voices had been lost. The period when children were taken from parents and forbidden to speak their native tongue and when native religious and doctoring rites had been forbidden had seen a loss of much knowledge.

The first written Shoshone narrative was that of Cameahwait, Sacajawea's brother. Strong native voices had since emerged in the Great Basin in favor of

civil rights legislation and social programs. The Shoshone and other Great Basin groups found tools to preserve their elders' wisdom and bring their concerns before others. The written word would both preserve traditional Shoshone culture and become a tool to protect Shoshone interests. Maryjane Ambler's recent book, *Breaking the Iron Bonds: Indian Control of Energy Development*, is dedicated, "To the young warriors of the energy tribes, who will take up the battle with law books and tribal codes as their weapons."

Native voices have emerged in newspapers such as the *Wind River Journal* and the *Sho-Ban News*. Shoshone authors have published tribal histories, and oral historians have videotaped Shoshone elders reciting the tales they learned around the fires of the piñon villages as children. These tapes—which preserve facial expressions, symbolic gestures, and nuances more vividly than the printed word—are watched by Shoshone children who attend reservation schools taught by Shoshone teachers.

The Shoshone remain masters of survival. They have met the challenges of modern American life while preserving their unique cultural identity. The same cultural flexibility that ensured their survival in one of the world's harshest environments guarantees that the Shoshone will continue to live as a unique and vibrant people in the Great Basin. ▲

BIBLIOGRAPHY

Clark, Ella Elizabeth, and Margot Edmonds. *Sacagawea of the Lewis and Clark Expedition.* Berkeley: University of California Press, 1979.

Crum, Steven J. *The Road on Which We Came: Po'i Pentun Tammen Kimmappeh.* Salt Lake City: University of Utah Press, 1994.

D'Azevedo, Warren L., ed. *Handbook of North American Indians: Great Basin,* vol. 11. Washington, D.C.: Smithsonian Institution, 1986.

Franklin, Robert J., and Pamela A. Bunte. *The Paiute.* New York: Chelsea House, 1990.

Hultkrantz, Ake. *Native Religions of North America.* San Francisco: Harper, 1987.

Lanner, Ronald M. *The Piñon Pine: A Natural and Cultural History.* Reno: University of Nevada Press, 1981.

Limerick, Patricia Nelson. *Desert Passages.* Albuquerque: University of New Mexico, 1985.

Madsen, Brigham D. *The Shoshone Frontier and the Bear River Massacre.* Salt Lake City: University of Utah Press, 1985.

——. *Chief Pocatello, the "White Plume."* Salt Lake City: University of Utah Press, 1986.

Rollings, Willard. *The Comanche.* New York: Chelsea House, 1989.

Steward, Julian H. "The Great Basin Shoshonean Indians." In *The North American Indians, A Sourcebook,* edited by R. C. Owen et al. New York: Macmillan, 1967.

THE SHOSHONE AT A GLANCE

TRIBE *Shoshone*

CULTURE AREA *Great Basin*

GEOGRAPHY *Great Basin/Great Plains area*

LINGUISTIC FAMILY *Numic branch of Uto-Aztecan family*

CURRENT POPULATION *Approximately 10,000*

FEDERAL STATUS *Tribal reservations in Idaho, Nevada, Utah, Wyoming, and California*

GLOSSARY

agent A person appointed by the Bureau of Indian Affairs to supervise U.S. government programs on a reservation or in a specific region.

allotment A U.S. government policy that broke up tribally owned reservations by assigning individual farms and ranches to Native Americans. Allotment was intended as much to discourage traditional communal activities as to encourage private farming and to assimilate Indians into mainstream American life.

archaeologist A scientist who studies past human societies through the objects, records, and settlements that people leave behind.

Bureau of Indian Affairs A federal government agency, now within the Department of the Interior, founded to manage relations with Native American tribes.

camas A type of lily with edible bulbs that grows in the western United States.

chuckwalla A type of large lizard caught by the Shoshone as food.

ecotone A transitional ecological zone where plants and animals from several distinct zones intermingle.

Great Basin An arid region of the United States that includes Utah and Nevada; western Colorado; southern Oregon, Idaho, and Wyoming; eastern California; and northern Arizona and New Mexico.

microenvironment A small, effectively isolated habitat with a distinct climate.

Numas A group of people who migrated to the Great Basin from the Southwest approximately a thousand years ago and are the ancestors of the Paiutes and the Shoshone.

piñon A low-growing pine tree of the American West that bears an edible seed; also, the seed of the piñon tree.

puhagan A Shoshone healer.

rainshadow An area of little rainfall located on the leeward side of a mountain range, created because the mountains block most rain clouds.

reservation A tract of land retained by Indians for their own occupation and use.

shaman A religious leader who acts as a healer, counselor, and diviner.

treaty A contract negotiated between nations.

tribe A society consisting of several separate communities united by kinship, culture, language, and other social institutions, including clans, religious organizations, and warrior societies.

vision quest A sacred ritual in which a man or an adolescent boy goes off alone for a set period of fasting and praying to receive revelations from supernatural spirits, who may act as personal guardians.

INDEX

KIM DRAMER teaches archaeology at Parsons School of Design, the New School for Social Research in New York City. She holds a Ph.D. in art history and archaeology from Columbia University. She has written several books on Native American culture and world history, and her articles on art, archaeology, and travel have appeared in numerous publications.

FRANK W. PORTER III, general editor of INDIANS OF NORTH AMERICA, is director of the Chelsea House Foundation for American Indian Studies. He holds a B.A., M.A., and Ph.D. from the University of Maryland. He has done extensive research concerning the Indians of Maryland and Delaware and is the author of numerous articles on their history, archaeology, geography, and ethnography. He was formerly director of the Maryland Commission on Indian Affairs and American Indian Research and Resource Institute, Gettysburg, Pennsylvania, and he has received grants from the Delaware Humanities Forum, the Maryland Committee for the Humanities, the Ford Foundation, and the National Endowment for the Humanities, among others. Dr. Porter is the author of *The Bureau of Indian Affairs* in the Chelsea House KNOW YOUR GOVERNMENT series.

PICTURE CREDITS

American Heritage Center, University of Wyoming: p. 43; American Museum of Natural History: p. 18; American Museum of Natural History, Department of Library Services: p. 78, neg. #316477; Arizona State Museum of Natural History: p. 18; Buffalo Bill Historical Center, Cody, WY, Vincent Mercaldo Collection: p. 60; Cell Prehistoric Museum: p. 28, photos by Pearl Oliver; Copyright: Christine Steeter: p.22; Denver Public Library, Western History Division: pp. 12, 46, 68, 70; Elko Daily Free Press: p. 88; Idaho Museum of Natural History: p. 16; Idaho State Historical Society: pp. 34-35, 39, 44, 73, 74; Illustration by Gary Tong: p. 2 (frontis); Illustration by Jack Malotte: pp. 80, 87; Joslyn Art Museum, Enron Art Foundation: p. 56 Nevada Historical Society: pp. 15, 83 Peabody Museum, Harvard University: pp. 21, photo by Hillel Burger, 23, photo by Hillel Burger, 24, photo by Hillel Burger, 31, 32; Smithsonian Institution, National Anthropological Archives: p. 26, photo by William H. Jackson; Special Collections Department, University of Nevada, Reno Library: p. 40; Special Collections, University of Utah Library: p. 67; State Historical Society of North Dakota: pp. 54, 55, 58; Utah State Historical Society: pp. 63, 77; Wyoming Division of Cultural Resources: pp. 36, 42; Wyoming State Museum: pp. 49, 50, 51, 52, photos by Craig Pindell; Yale University Library: p. 64.

CODMAN SQUARE